# Reflections for the Unfolding Year

# Reflections for the Unfolding Year

Alan Wilkinson

Ⓛ
The Lutterworth Press

**The Lutterworth Press**
P.O. Box 60
Cambridge
CB1 2NT
United Kingdom

www.lutterworth.com
publishing@lutterworth.com

ISBN: 978 0 7188 9498 6

*British Library Cataloguing in Publication Data*
A record is available from the British Library

In gratitude for the Church of England
Catholic, Reformed, Liberal

# Table of Contents

## II. Keeping Faith in God

# Preface

I enjoyed the privilege of being an honorary priest at the Cathedral of St Thomas of Canterbury, Portsmouth for twenty-six years until 2014. I was a Spiritual Director, Diocesan Theologian and a tutor for potential ordinands. I was also engaged in writing the centenary history of the Community of the Resurrection (1992), a study of Christian Socialism (1998), a novel about the monastic life, *One Foot in Eden* (2011), and contributed to several symposia. For some years I was a tutor for the Open University and then a Visiting Lecturer at Portsmouth University. My wife also enjoyed contributing to the life of the Cathedral. Members of the Cathedral sometimes asked for copies of my meditations given at the Sunday Sung Eucharist or Evensong. This appreciation encourages me to select fifty of those addresses – twenty-nine of them are reflections on the main events of the Christian Year as the drama unfolds, and twenty-one of them ponder recurring topics such as Remembrance Sunday, social justice, as well as the changing patterns of marriage and of biblical interpretation.

The earliest part of Portsmouth Cathedral, in simple Gothic, dates from 1185. After the destruction of the nave during the Civil War, its replacement was in a Classical style. In the 1930s, a new nave was built in a neo-Romanesque style. The west end was completed with its twin towers in the same style in 1991. Internally, the re-ordering drew the three different styles into a 'unity in diversity', through renewed Eucharistic worship, focussed on the altar round which we gathered after the ministry of the Word. The Cathedral, splendidly rejuvenated under David Stancliffe (later Bishop of Salisbury), bore witness to the character of the Church of England, which I have celebrated in my dedication as 'Catholic, Reformed, Liberal'; adjectives which I hope could also describe these reflections.

I am deeply indebted to Angharad Thomas for her editorial assistance.

*Alan Wilkinson,*
*Chichester, Easter 2017*

# I.
# Reflections on the Christian Year

# 1.
# Advent: The End and Endings

A few years ago, a photograph appeared in the 'Church Times' of a church notice board which announced: 'Advent: Jesus is coming.' Below it there was another sign: 'Police Notice. No waiting.'

At times Jesus seemed to have believed that he would return soon after his resurrection, as did Paul. In later parts of the New Testament, however, such expectations were modified. Yes, Jesus will come again, says Matthew 24, but only after the Gospel has been preached to all the nations. The first Christians quoted Malachi 4:1, which announces that the day is coming 'that shall burn like an oven', when the wicked will be punished. St Paul in 2 Thessalonians complained of having to deal with Christians so obsessed with the second coming that they had given up working. Paul tells them to get on with their ordinary lives instead. It is striking that Christians gripped by the original excitement about the second coming were now being told to get on with their day to day work.

The Bible does not conceive of history as cyclical, as Eastern religions do. Rather, for the Bible, history moves towards a goal. History has a meaning and a purpose. Evil and good will not forever co-exist. In the end there will be a great judgement, a great vindication of good, and God will reign. When Jesus came, then, early Christians saw him as the end, the goal, the meaning of it all.

History was going to end. The problem for the Church has always been that history *hasn't* ended. It was the imminent expectation of the end that gave Jesus and the early Christians their particular urgency and edge. The fact that Jesus has not returned has always been a great puzzle. You can't go on telling a child 'Your birthday is coming' in order to keep up their keen expectancy if their birthday never arrives. Down the centuries, various sects have arisen with the urgent message that 'Jesus is about to return'. The Jehovah's Witnesses, founded in 1870, proclaimed that Jesus would return invisibly in 1878. After 1878, their followers were told that in 1914 Jesus would return visibly and take the elect into God's kingdom, but 1914 came and went and Jesus was nowhere to be seen. Some argued that he did return, but you could only see him if you had true faith. More recently, a sect in Uganda formed themselves around the idea that Jesus would return in 2000. They were devastated when he did not. The core members all committed suicide. On one railway line I used to travel someone had painted on his roof that Jesus would return on such and such a date. But I noticed that he kept changing the date as one prediction after another failed.

When adventism (as it is called) attracts such odd people, why do we keep on proclaiming in creed and acclamation in the Eucharist that Christ will come again? If history is meaningless and without purpose then belief in a Last Judgement is pointless. Does life have a meaning, a goal or a purpose? If so, then the belief in a last judgement and second coming expresses this. History doesn't simply continue on without anything being resolved. Rowan Williams wrote in *Tokens of Trust* (98): 'All we need to know about the Last Judgement is that it will happen and that we don't know when. So we have to live in a state of constant preparedness to encounter complete truth.' An earlier theologian, Edwyn Hoskyns, said in a sermon: 'The one fundamental moral problem, is what we should still possess if the whole of our world was destroyed tomorrow, and we stood naked before God.' (*Cambridge Sermons.*)

But although the time of the Last Judgement is unknown, we have many other less dramatic moments ''that act as 'the end of a chapter': leaving junior school, leaving the choir, leaving school altogether, or leaving university or college. I was always very conscious of it when I was doing this or that for the last time. A friend said I was a 'connoisseur of last occasions'. I don't know whether that will count for or against me at the Last Judgement. Even weddings are always tinged with an element of pain, with parents and children letting go of one another to marry someone else who now will come first. Retirement is another obvious end. If you've become totally identified with your role you can feel totally stripped of your identity – as I know from having run pre-retirement courses for clergy and their wives. The Methodist minister and historian Gordon Rupp said in a sermon: 'Life has its own ways of setting examinations for us. . . . Around our Sixty Plus we meet a whole group of them – growing older, meeting pain and illness, separation and bereavement, death. . . . We are here to acknowledge the mysterious wisdom of God who is for ever disturbing, interrupting, breaking the patterns of our human loves, so that every handshake, every wave of the hand, every departure is the reminder that we are strangers and pilgrims and have here no abiding city.' (*The Sixty Plus and Other Sermons.*)

There are times when the apocalyptic biblical images of the end suddenly make sense to us. A theological student in Cambridge was studying the book of Revelation in September 1939. It hadn't meant very much to him at first, but when war broke out, it immediately came to have deep meaning and relevance.

The most obvious end is death. Dennis Potter, the controversial playwright, gave an astonishing interview to Melvyn Bragg in March 1994, a few weeks before he died of cancer. The fact that he was very near his end was emphasised by the bottle of morphine from which he took swigs from time to time. His nearness to his end heightened all his senses:

> In a perverse sort of way I'm almost serene, I can celebrate life. Below my window in Ross, for example the blossom is out in full. . . . And instead of saying 'Oh, that's nice blossom', looking at it through the window . . . it is the whitest, frothiest, blossomiest blossom that there ever could be . . . the nowness of everything is absolutely wondrous . . . the glory of it, if you like the comfort of it, the reassurance. . . . I see God in us or with us, if I see God at all, as shreds and particles and rumours, some knowledge that we have, some feeling why we sing and dance and act, why we paint, why we love, why we make art.
>
> *Dennis Potter,* Without Walls, *5 April 1994*

Reports like this from the end of the line carry conviction and hope for us as we reach our various smaller endings during life and, as we draw near to our own ends, our own deaths.

# 2.

# Advent: Judgement

Do you remember *Monty Python's Flying Circus*? At the very beginning a huge bare foot would often descend from heaven and crush a poor human being who was making some sort of protest. This is how some people regard God's judgement: as an arbitrary, sadistic and violent act. But although there are examples in the Old Testament where God's punishment comes across this way, it is quite clear that with Jesus, judgement is not arbitrary, but deeply moral. With Jesus, judgement has the purpose of goodness and godliness.

The New Testament asks a stark question: 'How do you respond to Jesus? If you don't know him, how do you respond to those values he embodies?' In St John's Gospel we read 'this is the judgement that the light has come into the world and people loved darkness rather than light' (3:19). Again and again the Gospel stories ask us: 'Where do you stand, whose side are you on, do you love light or darkness?' The Greek word for judgement is crisis – and that is how the New Testament writers saw the coming of Jesus. The coming of Jesus was a time of crisis, of judgement; a time when the alternatives are starkly laid out. Jesus needed John the Baptist to prepare the way for him. John came preaching that the crisis had come and that people must turn round and repent.

'Even now the axe is lying at the root of the tree' (John 3:19). Jesus had a winnowing tool in his hand to separate the wheat from the chaff (Matthew 3:10). Judgement is therefore not arbitrary, but the result of our actions. Judgement operates using the moral and physical laws that are built into our lives. A heavy smoker goes to the doctor complaining of a cough and chest pain; the doctor says bluntly: 'If you go on like this, you'll be dead in a few months.' The doctor is not punishing him, but simply pointing out the consequences of the man's actions. A crisis brings judgement and this can lead to repentance; a change of mind and direction.

We see this in Dickens' *A Christmas Carol*. Scrooge is forced to face his own cruelty and meanness. He is horrified when watching scenes from his life and repents. He send a turkey to his ill-used clerk, happily subscribes to Christmas charities and is no longer the old churlish miser he once was. A more modern writer, George Orwell, the author of *1984* and *Animal Farm*, thought that the major issue of his time was the decay of people's belief in life after death and their sense of being accountable to God, the judge of all.

I will give four examples to illustrate what I am trying to say.

(1) Peter Fisher, a good friend, describes his journey of faith in his fine book *Outside Eden* (2009). At one point, he tells the story of how, as a young priest, he neglected his family by working too hard. He went on a course about pastoral care. The course leader saw that there was something wrong with Peter. During the final session of the group, the leader told Peter to put his wife's name on a chair and tell her what he needed to say. He stumbled out his confession about his neglect of her. He then had to repeat the exercise when he got home, not to a chair but to his wife Elizabeth. It was humiliating, he says, but healing in the same way that good surgery is healing. When he confessed his neglect to his wife, he received both judgement and forgiveness.

(2) Judgement can take many different forms. A well-known teacher of management skills used to tell a story about how much he learned from one of his spectacular failures. As a young Shell executive in Malaysia, he came up with what he thought was a brilliant scheme. Instead of shipping oil up to the villages in drums, he decided to install storage tanks along the river that could then be filled by a tanker. It was only later that he realised he had made a colossal mistake. In the dry season the water level fell by one hundred feet. The tanker on the river could not possibly reach the storage tanks one hundred feet above. Out of that failure he learned humility, and he learned that his colleagues trusted him and respected him, so much so that they did not report him to head office. He learned to ask the opinions of other people instead of relying solely on his own judgement. Out of this crisis came a new beginning.

(3) An international conference on climate change is being held. It is a time of crisis, a time of judgement, a time to face the consequences of our way of life, and a time to repent, turn around. If we were told authoritatively that a meteorite five miles across would hit the earth on 5 December, everyone in the world would be clamouring for their governments to do something. Climate change is less obvious, more like a tide which at first comes in gradually, then gathers force and power.

Some people are already suffering from prolonged drought due to climate change. Some are suffering torrential rain storms. The sea is rising, so some people are having to evacuate low-lying islands and parts of Bangladesh. The poor are always the first to suffer for the greed of rich nations like ourselves. If each of us drove less and flew less, that would help. But our government will have to force us to make drastic changes in our lifestyles. If we don't change our habits and large parts of the Arctic ice melt, in my imagination I can see the sea breaking over a few yards from where we are now, and surging up the High Street and elsewhere along the front. I see people having to be rescued by helicopter and taken up to Portsdown Hill. Will we realise the crisis in time and repent?

(4) Human beings are like trees in the forest marked with a sign to indicate that eventually we are to be all cut down. Death is another form of crisis, with its attendant themes of judgement and repentance. In a hospice, a young, fashionable woman patient was slow to come to terms with her terminal illness. But a few days before she died, the nurse saw her take off her false eyelashes, her false hair piece and her false nails. She put them all in a drawer by her bed and said to the nurse: 'I don't think I shall need these any more.' The approach of death moved her into truth, into living with her real self. She had to stop pretending.

Advent carol services often begin in darkness. T.S. Eliot wrote in 'The Four Quartets': 'Every moment is a new and shocking valuation of all we have been.' When a crisis comes, in a relationship or in a business decision, as we face the fact of climate change, as we face the fact that we shall die, it is like a flash of lightning across a dark scene. We discover what we are made of, what we are made for, what sort of people we are, how our decisions in the past have made us what we have become. John the Baptist said of the coming Messiah: 'His winnowing fork is in his hand' (Luke 3:17). Advent is about crisis and judgement; about repentance before it is too late.

# 3.
# Advent: Penitence

The plane is just taking off. The ferry is just leaving harbour. Over the tannoy we hear: 'We are required to make the following safety announcement.' You are a seasoned traveller. You've heard it all before many times, and you show you are indeed a seasoned traveller by reading the newspaper and refusing to pay attention. Is that how we treat expressions of penitence in the services of the church? You've heard it many times before. Do the words no longer make any impact?

But what if the captain announced: 'I want you all to listen – this is a real emergency'? Then we'd listen to every word, because it was a matter of life or death. Isn't penitence a matter of life and death? A choice between life with God or spiritual death?

When we reach penitence in the liturgy, we ought to have prepared it beforehand by examining our lives this past week, instead of chatting to our neighbour. Oh, yes, there was that quarrel with bitter words; I have prayed so little; I've been indifferent to the sufferings of others; I didn't recycle my waste. Shouldn't we also be penitent on behalf of the whole world? We the human race 'have erred and strayed from thy ways like lost sheep'; we see it on the news and read about it in the papers every day. We offer penitence on behalf of the whole human race through those anguished Kyries at the beginning of some of the sung masses: 'Lord have mercy, Christ have mercy, Lord have mercy.'

Are we very confused about penitence? The Reformers in the 1662 Book of Common Prayer felt the urgent need to teach people that the Christian faith requires a moral response; it's not magic. The Prayer Book piles on heavily emotional language to shake us out of complacency: 'We acknowledge and bewail our manifold sins and wickedness . . . provoking most justly thy wrath and indignation against us . . . the burden of them is intolerable.' Modern penitential liturgy is less emotional and much shorter, but then penitence isn't primarily a matter of feeling. New Year resolutions are a secular form of penitence, and concentrate on one or two practical matters which need to be put right. If one is always late for work, it's no good to beat one's breast and cry, 'What a dreadful person I am.' Real penitence in that case means going out to buy a good alarm clock. New Year resolutions are often refreshingly down to earth and practical.

Why are modern Christians confused about how to express their penitence? Has there been a decline in penitence towards God? The secular idea of penitence is often expressed in a self-centred way: 'I've let myself down.' By contrast, the Christian understanding of penitence is focussed outwardly on God and other people: 'I've let God down, let the church down, let my friends and neighbours down, let the saints down.' Advent used to focus on the Four Last Things: heaven, hell, death, and judgement. Taking penitence seriously is in line with the traditional understanding of Advent, which today is often neglected.

Do we feel a sense of awe about facing God? When we die, do we expect to saunter in, hands in pockets for nothing more than a cosy chat? We have much less sense now that each one of us is a sinner accountable to God day by day, and that each of us will one day have to give an account of our stewardship, how we have used the gifts and opportunities we have been given. Are we also confused about how responsible we are for our sins? There are two very different extreme attitudes that one might take. 'It's all my fault', perhaps, or 'I'm simply a victim of the system, of my upbringing'. Of course, we can never work out precisely how responsible we are for our wrong-doing. But penitence includes realistic and mature owning up. There is an old story of a man making his confession to a priest. 'Father, I found a rope.' The priest responds: 'That doesn't sound very serious.' 'Ah, but Father, you see, there was a horse at the end of it.' Taking responsibility is a sign of maturity.

Sacramental confession is one form of penitence neglected by Anglicans: that is to say, a confession to God in the presence of a priest. In the Revised Catechism it is one of the seven ministries of the church. In the first of the long exhortations in the 1662 Prayer Book in the service of Holy Communion, the priest says that if you cannot quieten your own conscience, go to him or some other priest 'that by the ministry of God's Holy Word you may receive the benefit of absolution, together with ghostly [i.e. spiritual] counsel and advice'.

In the service for the Visitation of the Sick, the sick person is encouraged to make a confession of sin if he feels himself troubled with any weighty matter. It provides a stirring form of absolution: 'Our Lord Jesus Christ, who hath left power to his church to absolve all sinners who truly repent and believe in him, of his great mercy forgive thee thine offences. And by his authority committed to me, I absolve thee from all thy sins, in the Name of the Father and of the Son, and of the Holy Ghost. Amen.'

There are few more moving and marvellous moments in the ministry of priests than when they say these words to a penitent. At their ordination priests are given the power and authority to absolve. Many Anglicans are sadly ignorant of this sacramental ministry. Yet the Church of England has provided new helpful forms of sacramental confession in the new liturgies. Some Anglicans make their confessions on the eve of some great event – marriage or ordination, or when they have got into a terrible mess, or during a serious illness, or before death. Some make their confessions more regularly, once a year at Christmas or Easter.

What are the advantages of sacramental confession? (1) It is very Godward – like an acted prayer. (2) It is very specific – not just feeling rather bad in a vague way but the confessing and repenting of specific sins. (3) I receive advice and comment directed to me personally in my specific situation. (4) What is said is in total confidence: all is under the 'seal of the confessional'. (5) By using this ministry I realise that by my failure to pray, my failure to be honest in business and so on, I am weakening the army of God in our fight against evil. We are all fellow members of the Body of Christ, dependent upon one another. It is appropriate to confess to God and the whole company of heaven in the presence of a priest who represents God and the community.

In the early 1950s, I was an undergraduate in Cambridge. We were blessed to receive a mission to the university led by Michael Ramsey, then Archbishop of York, later of Canterbury. He was the greatest and most saintly Archbishop of the twentieth century. In one address he said:

I commend to you what is called 'going to confession' or 'sacramental confession', the method whereby you confess your sins audibly in the presence of the priest and receive from him audibly Christ's absolution. The Church of England offers this way of confession and absolution to those who voluntarily choose it. It is a method thorough, painful, decisive, full of comfort. The priest is no barrier: rather does his ministry enable you to find Christ near in his own vivid forgiveness.

*Introducing the Christian Faith, 55*

At the beginning of a new Christian year, it is good to ask ourselves about one of the basics of Christian life: penitence. How much does it mean to us? What can we do to make it real? What do all those penitential words in the liturgy really mean as we say them? Would it help me if I began to use the sacramental ministry of penitence?

# 4.
# Advent: Mary the Pilgrim

There are ten pictures in Portsmouth Cathedral of the same person. Isn't that extraordinary? Who is it? There are two in the east window, four in St Thomas' chapel, two icons, one banner, and one Della Robbia plaque. Today, on the Sunday before Christmas, we celebrate the woman who made Christmas possible.

Mary is sometimes called the new Eve, because Eve disobeyed and said 'No', but Mary said 'Yes'. Adam shifted all the blame onto Eve, you remember: 'The woman you put here with me – she gave me some fruit from the tree, and I ate it' (Genesis 3:12). There is a long history of blaming women, of men fearing women, of women being excluded and forgotten. After Jesus had fed a large crowd, St Matthew tells us that 'those who had eaten were four thousand men beside women and children'. Note that women and children were regarded as not worth counting. Were there perhaps fifteen thousand people in reality? When Jane Hedges was one of the Canons here (she is now Dean of Norwich), she celebrated her first Eucharist after she was priested in 1994. I went back to my seat after receiving communion from her and that text from Genesis sprang to mind: 'The woman gave me and I ate.' That long history of women being despised and excluded was coming to an end.

The priesting of women encouraged a new type of devotion to Mary. So often Mary had been portrayed as a passive and docile woman, but now we began to see her in a very different light. Rowan Williams, the former Archbishop of Canterbury, has pointed out that Mary was the first person to put her trust in God as shown in Jesus. He describes Mary as an older sister who holds our hand to help us walk towards Jesus.

I want to suggest three aspects of Mary to ponder as we approach Christmas Day.

## 1. *Mary Our Fellow Pilgrim*

As you approach Salisbury Cathedral, you see a figure walking away. This is the statue of the Walking Mary. She is gaunt and thin, middle aged. She has clearly gone through a great deal since she was that young girl at the Annunciation. At the Annunciation she had to move from bewilderment to acceptance of an unknown and sometimes painful future. Then there was the time when Jesus as a young boy went missing in Jerusalem. Mary and Joseph found him in the Temple. He explained that he had a higher loyalty: 'Did you not know that I must be in my Father's House?' (Luke 2:49.) Do you remember his cool rebuke to Mary at Cana? (John 2:4.) Or the occasion when he was too busy with the crowd to attend to her and his family? Mary and his brothers had come to take him away. He responds: 'Who are my mother and my brothers? . . . Whoever does the will of God is my brother and sister and mother.' (Mark 3:33-35.)

All the time she was learning to be a pilgrim. She had to keep moving on and learn to respond to often bewildering experiences. In the end, it was this which enabled her to stand beneath his cross. From the cross, Jesus says to us and all believers: 'Here is your mother' (John 19:27). Do you think of Mary as your mother in Christ? From time to time in this cathedral we start in the nave and then move up into the choir. We have to leave the comfort of the seats we have picked for ourselves and move on in a kind of pilgrimage, not knowing where we shall sit. Advent and Christmas call us to be pilgrims with Mary.

## 2. *Mary the Prophet of Liberation*

In Latin America and elsewhere in recent decades, Mary is celebrated, especially by the poor, as a prophet of liberation. She prophesises a new order; a new value system. People aren't valued by God, she says, because of their wealth or social position, but because of their faith. 'He has brought down the powerful from their thrones, and lifted up the lowly' – words spoken or sung daily in our churches in the Magnificat (Luke 1:52).

Do we believe the revolutionary vision of the Magnificat? Do you remember what passage from Scripture Jesus used when he first addressed the congregation in the synagogue at Nazareth? 'The Spirit of the Lord is upon me because he has anointed me to bring good news to the poor . . . release to the captives . . . to let the oppressed go free.' Having read this, Jesus said: 'Today this Scripture has been fulfilled in your hearing.' (Luke 18:21.) Note how Jesus echoes his mother's words. Ponder the fact that there was no room for Mary, Joseph and Jesus at the inn. The so-called wise men sought for Jesus in the capital city, in the royal palace. That was the natural place to look, but in the end they found him among animals in a stable. The whole Christmas story is deeply subversive – it turns our scale of values upside down.

This is the divine comedy: like those old Charlie Chaplin films where the self-important man slips on a banana skin and fall flat on his face. He despises Charlie, the little shabby man on the kerb. The film echoed the Magnificat: the humble and meek have been exalted. Mary, the prophet of liberation, turns everything upside down.

## 3. 'Mary treasured all these words and pondered them in her heart'; 'His mother treasured all these things in her heart.'

St Luke describes Mary in almost identical terms twice in his second chapter. Is it strange that Mary the pilgrim and the subversive prophet is also Mary the contemplative? Those who ponder experience, and see it from a Godward viewpoint, see life in a subversive way. The contemplative spirit detaches them from the values of this world, making them less likely to conform. 'How silently, how silently the wondrous gift is given,' we sing at Christmas. Silence here is very subversive. It exposes what is real.

On a silent retreat a fortnight ago, I spent some time gazing at an old sheep in the rain. Normally I would have hurried by, preoccupied with my own affairs. Noise and busyness desensitise us so that we no longer hear or see properly. I stayed in a monastery once where the services were punctuated by prolonged periods of attentive silence. A few verses of a psalm, then silence. A few verses from a Gospel, then silence. A hymn, then silence. I was reminded of Psalm 131: 'I have quieted and stilled my soul, like a weaned child on its mother's breast.'

Too often even church services are as busy and rushed as the world outside. We are told twice in the second chapter of St Luke's Gospel that Mary didn't rush through her experiences. Rather, she took it out like a precious stone and looked at it from every side: 'Mary kept all these things and pondered them in her heart.' Mary our fellow pilgrim; Mary the subversive; Mary the contemplative.

> O God the source of all insight, whose coming was revealed to the nations not among men of power, but on a woman's lap, give us grace to seek you where you may be found, that the wisdom of this world may be humbled and discover your unexpected joy, through Jesus Christ our Lord. Amen.                    *Janet Morley*

# 5.

# How the Christmas Story Developed

We are here because two thousand years ago a young woman said yes to God. She could have said no. Had other women refused? There was a mysterious young woman mentioned in Isaiah, 'the young woman is with child and will bear a son and shall name him Immanuel'. ('God with us', Isaiah 7:14.) The Greek version of the verse describes the young woman as a virgin. Matthew quoted this in its Greek form and so helped solidify the belief in the virgin birth of Jesus (1:23). The whole history of the human race climaxes in this 'Yes' of Mary: a moment celebrated by poets and artists ever since.

We should think also of her parents, who are traditionally thought to be Anne and Joachim (they are now celebrated by the Church of England on 26 July each year). We should be grateful for all that they gave Mary by their example and prayer. Their choices influenced her choices. And her grandparents – what of them, or her great-grandparents, or her other relations and friends? All these totally obscure people through their faith and choices influenced Mary's choices. As a woman she was considered inferior in her society. She lacked the status of motherhood. But, as in a pantomime, or as in Dickens' *A Christmas Carol*, the mighty are put down and the humble are exalted. This is the beginning of the great topsy-turvy world prophesied in Mary's 'Magnificat' (Luke 1:46f) and enacted by Jesus in the Gospel stories.

There is also development in the New Testament itself. The earlier writers, like Paul and Mark, did not mention the nativity stories. Either they did not know them or they did not think they were important. It was only later that Gospel writers such as Luke and Matthew told stories about the nativity. For Matthew and Luke, the story of the virgin birth expressed the belief that Jesus wasn't just an especially good man produced by holy parents. No, Jesus was born as the result of God's initiative combined with Mary's generous co-operation. This is the meaning of the virgin birth. Christians have gone on meditating about the significance of the nativity ever since – in writings, paintings, music, poetry, and plays. For the first three centuries, Christians regarded Easter as the climax of the Christian year. But by the 300s Christians began to affirm their belief through the Nicene Creed that Jesus was 'God from God, light from light'. That belief was turned into a celebration. Christians took over the Roman feast of the 'Unconquered Sun', which took place on 25 December. By 25 December, we realise that the days are getting longer again: the sun (Son) has not been conquered. Jesus was indeed 'light for those who sit in darkness' (Luke 1:79).

Through Christian meditation on the nativity over the centuries, our understanding of it has developed. Take the theme dear to modern people – the baby Jesus. In the ancient world, children were insignificant and had few rights. It was not until the Franciscans in the thirteenth century that Christians turned their attention to the child Jesus. Books of devotion began to urge Christians in their imaginations to take the baby Jesus into their arms. Matthew and Luke would have found this idea incomprehensible. St Francis in 1223 may have been the first to create a crib scene and he included a live ox and live ass, although an ox and ass do not appear there in the Gospels. People thought that the word 'stable' inevitably implied animals being there and remembered the ox and ass mentioned in Isaiah (1:3). It was also Francis who first portrayed the family as poor. This was how Francis taught us to think tenderly of the holy family.

Artists followed the same pattern. One showed the infant Jesus playing with his mother's veil. By the Middle Ages pictures began to portray Mary's parents at the crib – the older generation needed to feel included, too. Jesus was for everyone. Look at your Christmas cards – there are the ox and the ass, never mentioned in the Gospels. There are the three kings – but Matthew actually describes them as astrologers or wise men. They found a verse in Psalms (72:10) to provide Scriptural backing. Why three? This was deduced from the three gifts. They were thought of as kings from about 200 CE. Their names, Caspar, Melchior and Balthasar, first appear around 500 CE. The belief that they represented three races developed by 1000 CE or so. The shepherds literally took centre stage in the mediaeval mystery plays, which reworked the Gospel stories in a down-to-earth fashion. Shepherds represented the ordinary people. In these plays, the shepherds complained about their wives, used crude words, did not understand Latin, and one was a thief. Even midwives began to appear in some crib scenes. The message was powerfully taught that Jesus came for sinners, for everyone. Stories were told about how the animals kept the baby Jesus warm. Bit by bit Christians came to believe that the whole of creation was there to worship and care for the child.

Carols often put us in touch with these reworkings of the stories. We can understand why then, though it is theologically correct to claim that Holy Week and Easter are the centre of the faith, the popular imagination has taken over the Christmas stories and made them into popular down-to-earth folk tales. This development was not approved of by all Christians. Cromwell and the Puritans in the seventeenth century abolished the Church of England, the Prayer Book and Christmas itself. On Christmas Day 1657, the diarist John Evelyn and his family discovered a church that was illegally using the Prayer Book and celebrating Christmas, but the church was surrounded by Cromwell's troops. When the Evelyn family went up to the altar to receive communion, soldiers pointed muskets at them.

In the mid-nineteenth century, the writer Edmund Gosse's father was a member of the Puritan group the Plymouth Brethren. In their household Christmas was forbidden. The very *word* was forbidden for being too Popish. But the servants disobeyed and made a Christmas pudding. They gave the young Edmund a piece. Unfortunately, because he disobeyed his father he developed a violent stomach ache. He sobbed: 'Oh! Papa, Papa, I have eaten of flesh offered to idols!' His father responded: 'Where is the accursed thing?' When he discovered it, he took it out and put it onto the dustheap, and raked this 'idolatrous confectionery' into the ashes (*Father and Son*, 64).

The reinterpretation of the Christmas story has continued into our own times. Many Christians who neglected Mary have rediscovered her. We have made the holy family fleeing to Egypt into asylum seekers. Their poverty illustrated by the birth at the inn has been used to stir our consciences about the poor today in our own world. A new carol fifty years ago described the birth as taking place in the waiting room of Huddersfield station in West Yorkshire – presumably the worst fate the composer could imagine.

I have tried to show how each Christmas our hearts and imaginations have been stirred by the Gospel stories. Our hearts and imaginations have also been stirred by the additions and interpretations through which Christians have enriched us over the centuries. Ponder the great pictures on our Christmas cards and kneel at the crib. As we come to communion, let us remember that this is the same Jesus who lay there in the stable. Let us thank God for Mary. For musicians and artists, for ordinary people who have used their imaginations to bring the stories down to earth. Let us thank God for St Francis and the first cribs; for pagans who taught us how to celebrate with mistletoe; for Prince Albert who brought us German customs, including Christmas trees; for Dickens'

*A Christmas Carol*; for carols old and new. We also thank God for that first English carol service at Truro Cathedral in 1880. We are thankful for King's College, Cambridge for making it popular through the radio after the First World War, in which its Dean had been an army chaplain. This service of Nine Lessons and Carols spread to every corner of the country, and is still an essential part of Christmas. It enables many who are on the edges of the church (as well as regular communicants) to feel sustained by both mainline Scripture as well as by folk interpretations of the incarnation created over the centuries in carols. This is what it means to say 'The Word became flesh and lived among us' (John 1:14).

# 6.

# Preparing for Christmas

In the beginning was the Word. . . . The Word became flesh and lived among us. . . .

*John 1:1-14*

In November my wife and I flew to Hong Kong to stay with family for a fortnight. From time to time we watched a map which showed the progress of the plane on the long flight. The flight map came in two versions. The first version of the map showed a large plane and a local map, so we could raise the blind and say 'Look, there is Warsaw'. The other version of the map showed a tiny plane and the whole map of the journey from London to Hong Kong. It's a little like that with the Gospels. In St Mark's Gospel there are no stories of the birth of Jesus at all. He places Jesus in a local context by quoting Isaiah to represent the Jewish tradition. When we turn to St Matthew's Gospel, we discover a long genealogy of Jesus showing how he was descended from Abraham, the father of the Jewish people. That extends the story further than Mark, but it is still confined to Jewish history. St Luke's Gospel, however, traces the genealogy of Jesus back to the beginning to Adam, the first man in Genesis, making Jesus both local (that is, Jewish), and universal (representing the whole human race). St John's Gospel was the last to be written and he starts at a much earlier point. We don't begin with stories about John the Baptist like Mark, nor do we begin with Abraham as with Matthew, nor with Adam as in Luke. But we start at the very beginning – 'In the beginning was the Word'. Those tremendous words echo the first words of Genesis. John places Jesus into a cosmic setting – the Word became flesh, but before that the Word was involved in the creation.

When I was a child in the 1930s, on 24 May, Empire Day, we were shown a large map of the world at school. A quarter of the globe was coloured red to show that it was part of the British Empire. When we were recently in Hong Kong, we were reminded of that Empire and the way in which, after 1945, nation after nation gained independence. We went to Hong Kong Cathedral on the Sunday. Outwardly it looked like a relic of Empire – built in a nineteenth century Gothic style. But the Eucharist was presided over by a Chinese Archbishop and a Chinese Dean. Of the fifty-six candidates for baptism and confirmation, all but three had Chinese names. We discovered that services were held in Filipino, Mandarin and Cantonese as well as in English. As we all know, Hong Kong was once part of the British Empire, and is now part of China with some degree of autonomy. When I was a child, Britain was the leading power in the world. After 1945, the United States became the dominant world power, a position that has been challenged by China and India in recent years. We can see a similar shift in the Anglican Communion. At one time the majority of Anglicans lived in Britain, but now the majority of Anglicans are brown or black and live in Africa and Asia. In our Bible story books, Jesus is still depicted as a white Englishman. In Asia, he is portrayed as Asian. In some African story books he is black. In our global world, Jesus must be presented as a man for everyone, for every race.

As far as St John's Gospel is concerned, Jesus is not a national figure belonging to one race. He is not God's afterthought; he is the flesh and blood expression of God's eternal Word which goes right back to the very beginning. 'In the beginning was the Word', St John's Gospel says. In the beginning was the meaning of all things, the purpose of all things, God expressing himself through his Word, the agent of God in creation: 'All things came into being through him.' It is significant that John drew this concept of the eternal Word from one of those books sandwiched between the Old and New Testaments – the book of Wisdom. Those books between the two Testaments are sometimes called the Apocrypha. They were deeply influenced by Greek culture. The book of Wisdom, written a hundred years before the birth of Jesus, was designed to appeal to Greeks and to show them the Jewish faith in a form that made sense in their culture. John in this majestic first chapter is breaking with Jewish nationalism to show that Jesus is of universal significance. Jesus is not only significant to Jews. He is the universal Word made flesh. Jesus is God making himself accessible and credible for the whole human race.

'The true light which enlightens everyone was coming into the world,' John wrote of the Word made flesh in Jesus. In this country, one of the benefits of immigration is that it has brought representatives of the whole world through our front door. Immigration has brought us not only vibrant new forms of Christianity from what used to be our Empire, but also temples and mosques. We are therefore forced to ask 'How do we know what is true in religion? How can we better understand Islam, for example?' This is question we face each Christmas when Muslims join us here in this cathedral to celebrate the birth of Jesus.

William Temple, who was the Archbishop of Canterbury during the Second World War, wrote a commentary on St John's Gospel, in which he was particularly struck by verse nine of the first chapter: 'The true light which enlightens everyone was coming into the world.' He said that all that is noble in other religions is the work of the Word of God, whether it is Isaiah or Buddha: 'There is only one divine light; and every man in his measure is enlightened by it.' The first chapter of St John's Gospel thus provides a vital message for our world of many cultures and religions. The Word made flesh in Jesus is the source of whatever truth or whatever light is to be found, wherever it is. He is the light which enlightens everyone; not just Christians, but everyone. That is an aspect of Christmas we easily overlook.

# 7.

# Epiphany: The Baptism of Jesus

John the baptiser appeared in the wilderness, proclaiming a baptism of repentance for the forgiveness of sins.

*Mark 1:4*

A baptism of repentance? What did it mean? Isn't repentance about turning to face another way and towards someone who will change you? As baptised people we are committed to a life of repentance. In the baptism service we are asked whether we will turn to Christ. 'Do you turn to Christ?'

I wonder whether you go back to your old school, college or university for reunions. I am not a great goer-back myself, but I do go back to my old college in Cambridge from time to time. I often meet people whom I knew when I was a student or later when I was the chaplain. Obviously they have changed, as I have. Probably snow has descended on what hair remains. People have changed in their characters too. I think of one who as a student fifty years ago was a shy, very academic, diffident young man. How did it happen that, fifty years later, he has become confident, outgoing, and warm? When I met his wife, I understood why he had changed. Her warmth, love for and confidence in her husband had drawn him out of his shy, isolated self so he could go out and speak confidently to other people.

A baptism for repentance, a turning to Christ. John was preparing a group to respond to Jesus. For them their baptism was about repentance. The baptism of Jesus: what did that mean? Jesus' baptism was more like an ordination to ministry. God declared: 'You are my Son, the Beloved; with you I am well pleased.' (Luke 3:22.) But for everyone else, baptism was about repentance: a turning round to face another way. But for us it isn't just a turn around. It is a turning to face Jesus: a turning so that through our relationship with him he can influence us, as that shy young man was drawn out of his isolation by the love of his wife and children.

When we are in a relationship that we cherish, we try to avoid doing anything which harms or breaks up that relationship. So it is with Jesus. If we are really seeking to grow in relationship with Jesus, our first priority becomes the fostering of that relationship. He gives us a new way of living life; a new way of being human.

Newly married couples often receive advice from priest or well-wishers, such as: 'Never go to sleep bearing a grudge. Say sorry before the grudge harms your relationship.' A marriage, a partnership or a friendship involves a regular pattern of returning to restore the relationship. At the end of the parable, the Prodigal Son says, 'I will get up and go to my father' (Luke 15:18). This is the purpose of prayer and sacraments. Each time we pray; each time we come to the Eucharist, we can say like the Prodigal Son, 'I will get up and go to my father.' It is baptism that begins the process of returning – we are born egotistical and self-centred, but God is the centre of all things, not oneself. It takes a lifetime to realise this; to move from being self-centred to being centred on God: that is the turning and the repentance he asks of us.

Do you remember particular points in your life when you turned around and faced towards Jesus? For me there were two major turnings round. One was when as a student I was confirmed and made my first confession to a priest; the second major turning around was when I was ordained. For some people the turning round, repentance, is a bit like falling in love, it is sudden and unexpected. Others grow towards a loving relationship with another human being almost imperceptibly – but usually there are points along the way when you make a venture and it seems to be worthwhile. You go out for the day together for the first time and it turns out well, even marvellously. What has your experience been of turning towards Jesus? Sometimes it is a hard struggle to let go of a way of life that is incompatible with following Jesus. In Shakespeare's play *Hamlet*, King Claudius wants to pray and is full of remorse – he feels guilty, but he cannot let go what he has gained through his sin. He has murdered his brother to get the throne and married his brother's widow. Claudius prays thus:

> But, O, what form of prayer
> Can serve my turn? 'Forgive me my foul murder'?
> That cannot be, since I am still possess'd
> Of those effects for which I did the murder,
> My crown, mine own ambition, and my queen.

*III.iii*

John the Baptist, according to Luke, was not only concerned with the repentance of individuals but with repentance in society. He explained to three different groups the meaning of repentance.

1.  Share your clothes and food with those who have none. Society should be about neighbourliness and sharing. Do you put food into the cathedral box for the poor and asylum seekers? Studies show that the most unequal societies are also the most unhappy. Great disparities in wealth, education and opportunities produce envy, conflict and depression. The present crisis bears most painfully upon the poorest. If the wealthy were willing to receive less and to help the poor, we would become a society of neighbours. How has it come about that we need to have food banks with collection points in supermarkets and churches?

2.  John the Baptist told the tax collectors: 'Collect no more than is due to you.' Don't exploit people over whom you have power (Luke 3:13f). In our day, banks have been lending money to people who had little or no ability to repay. It was cruel to raise their hopes falsely only to land them in debt and threaten them with the probable repossession of their homes.

3.  John the Baptist said to the soldiers: 'Do not extort money from anyone by threats' and 'be satisfied with your wages' (Luke 3:14). Again, he is saying: don't use intimidation to line your own pockets. Be satisfied with satisfied with the money you earn. However, our society depends upon making people perpetually discontented and dissatisfied. 'Be content' is not something we ever hear. Once we were content to have shops open six days a week. But now we think we ought to be able to shop seven days a week. If parents are working, then Sunday family lunch is destroyed. The fact that on one day a week shops were closed conveyed an important message: that there is more to life than acquisition. A society built around acquisition functions through making us dissatisfied. We are constantly told that unless we have this or that, then we will be unhappy, old-fashioned, despised, and, above all, dissatisfied.

Of course, there is a true discontent: a deep desire for peace in Gaza or justice in Zimbabwe, a discontent with our very unequal society. If you watched the adaptation of Dickens' novel *Little Dorrit* on television, did you see it as a parable for our times? In the novel, people live in various types of prison – William Dorrit is imprisoned for debt, like Dickens' father was; others are imprisoned by the endless search for an easy way to make money; imprisoned by the psychological damage of living in such a society; or imprisoned by religious bigotry. Dickens argues that in such a society ordinary human happiness is virtually impossible. George Bernard Shaw described *Little Dorrit* as a more seditious book than Karl Marx's manifesto *Das Kapital*. John the Baptist, like Dickens, says we're all to blame. He calls for communal as well as individual repentance. Portsmouth Cathedral is unusual in having a statue of St John the Baptist. Stand before him and ask what it might mean for you to undergo a baptism for repentance.

In today's collect we thank God for John the Baptist who was 'sent to prepare the way of your Son our Saviour by the preaching of repentance: leading us to repent according to his teaching'. Therefore let us ponder what this means to us as a society and as individuals.

# 8.
# Epiphany: The Wedding at Cana

Two of the lessons today are about the absurdly generous nature of God. In the first lesson from Kings 17, the widow has no food because of a drought. She and her son are preparing to die of starvation. But Elijah tells her that God will provide oil and flour until the rains come. God will provide food not just for today and tomorrow, but for days and weeks into the future. What historical basis the story has we do not know – it sounds very much like a folk tale. Folk tales often teach profound truths.

The Gospel story of the wedding feast at Cana from John 2 is again about the extraordinary generosity of God. When the wine runs out, Jesus provides not just a few more bottles. No: he produces a hundred and eighty gallons of fine wine. Again, it's not easy to know what historical basis the story has. Some think it a parable that has been turned into an incident, or another folk tale (like some of the parables are). Above all, John wants us to be amazed at the extravagant generosity of God.

The Cana story should remind of us the collect for Trinity 12: 'You are always more ready to hear than we to pray and to give more than we desire or deserve.' More than we desire. We pray: 'Lord send us two or three bottles to save the party' and he sends us a hundred and eighty gallons. We know that it's true sometimes for us, too. When we take our child in our arms for the first time. When someone tells us that we are loved. When we come through some frightening experience of pain and anguish. When we hear the words of God's forgiveness from a priest after we have made our first confession. When on the first day of Spring we see the crocuses, the leaves beginning to appear on the trees, the warmth of the returning sun, the birds singing. The Cana story echoes the Eucharist. Think of the gallons of wine poured into chalices over the centuries and the life of Christ given to us through the cup, much more than we either desire or deserve. We hold out our hands for a small glass of wine and he gives us a hundred and eighty gallons. At the heart of the

Christian faith is Gratitude, for that is what the word Eucharist means. 'Let us give thanks to the Lord our God.' I could easily end the sermon with that and we could go on to sing 'All things bright and beautiful'. But we know that there are other sides to life.

One of the things we have to learn is that we cannot measure goodness in the same way that we measure a gallon of wine. A small measure of love has more power than a huge amount of evil. The evening before the crucifixion, Jesus instituted the Eucharist in the Upper Room by giving thanks over bread and wine. Amazingly, he gave thanks. At the moment when, in human terms, Jesus was empty, run out, like the wine at Cana, God gave him strength, courage, and love so that he could triumph. It was as the nails were hammered into the hands of Jesus that he prayed, 'Father, forgive them, for they do not know what they are doing.' We see how terrible cruelty can produce extraordinary forgiveness. After one of the German concentration camps was liberated, a scrap of paper written by a prisoner was found. It asked God to forgive those who were operating the camp and its ovens for gassing the Jews.

At the end of April 1945, Harold Macmillan (later Prime Minister) was in Assisi, Italy, where St Francis had been born in 1181. Macmillan mused about all that this humble, powerless man had achieved, not just over his lifetime but down the centuries. (Remember, we have Franciscan friars and sisters in the Church of England today.) Macmillan was in Assisi just as the Germans were suing for peace. Later he remembered how he had walked in the valley bathed with moonlight and reflected on the war ending. He wrote: 'Hitler has lasted twelve years with all his powers of evil, his strength, his boasting. St Francis did not seem to have much power, but here in this lovely place, one realises the immense strength and permanence of goodness.' There is a fundamental unexpectedness about the Christian faith. It turns everything upside down. The hundred and eighty gallons of wine no doubt dumbfounded the people in charge of the wedding.

Many of you have seen the fine and moving film *The King's Speech*. I can remember on the one hand the splendid grandiloquence of Churchill's wartime broadcasts, but also how we sat on the edge of our chairs listening to every word King George VI spoke, willing him on to the next word. The words meant so much more because they came out of struggle, pain and humiliation.

Michael Mayne was a very distinguished Dean of Westminster Abbey and the author of some remarkable books about faith and experience. Soon after he began to write what turned out to be his last book, it was discovered he had cancer of the jaw. He was in the operating theatre for fifteen hours. He called his 2006 book *The Enduring Melody,* which is what musicians call the cantus firmus. Bach starts with the basic melody, then decorates it, turns it upside down, but in the end always comes back to the cantus firmus. In his book Michael Mayne was determined to give this new experience of cancer his full attention. Then he could name the God who was with him in it especially by surrounding him with the care of the hospital staff and the love and prayers of family and friends. With the exception of when he was heavily sedated after the operation, every day he said the liturgy of morning prayer and tried to hang onto a phrase from one of the psalms or Gospel readings. He prayed each morning (28): 'This is the day which the Lord has made; this is the place where I must look for him.' But the cancer returned. On the last pages of the book he faced his death. He said that if life was a gift, death too was a gift. We must let go of what we have been given. 'To die with gratitude for all that has been, without resentment for what you are going through and with openness to the future, is the greatest gift we can leave those who love us and who are left behind' (251). His final words in the book are of gratitude for the ordered rhythm of the seasons: the return of the swifts, the woods dappled with blossom, the hedgerows hung with May; all bearing witness to the annual pattern of death and new life; the enduring melody, the cantus firmus.

We come back to that phrase from the collect for Trinity: 'You give more than either we desire or deserve.'

# 9.
# Epiphany: Candlemass

On this lovely feast day, we celebrate the occasion when Mary and Joseph took Jesus to the Temple to present him to the Lord. They were too poor to offer a lamb for sacrifice, but offered instead a couple of birds. It's a story rich in poetry. My reflection today is going to be meditations with a short silence at the end of each, for us to ponder and pray.

Simeon and Anna were watching and waiting. Imagine you are at Gatwick waiting and watching for a young couple with a baby you've never seen before. The crowds flock through the barrier. Then you spot them – or those you think might be them – poor, not very well dressed, looking a bit bewildered and overawed. Pretend you are Simeon or Anna. Taught by the Scriptures, you've been looking for the coming of the Messiah all your life, fasting and praying, coming in and out of the temple, watching the crowds, looking for someone – but who? And how will you recognise him when he comes? Simeon and Anna knew the psalms: 'We wait for your loving kindness, O God in the midst of your temple' (Psalm 48). Is this cathedral a place where we wait for God to make himself known? 'We wait for your loving kindness, O God, in the midst of your temple.' Can we say that? Can we pray for that?

The other day a Polish man came into the cathedral. He walked round prayerfully and said to the guide as he went out, 'What a beautiful cathedral – but where are the people?' It was a good and disturbing question. He expected to see clusters of people praying and lighting candles. Why aren't there? One reason is that people say 'God is everywhere'. That is true, but there are places that are like a magnifying glass which focuses and intensifies the sun. Holy places can act as sacraments that focus and make available God's presence. Is that people don't come here because they don't know how to pray? Or perhaps they don't believe in God or praying? I once took a visitor into the great monastic church at Mirfield, West Yorkshire. He was overwhelmed by the atmosphere of prayer. He said: 'It seems to pray by itself; it seems to be attending to God.' Could we say that about this cathedral? We went once to visit the tomb of St Clare in Assisi. Large numbers of people were waiting there; there was absolute and attentive silence. Kierkegaard, the Danish philosopher, said that if we want to do anything, first procure silence. Let us spend a moment thinking of Anna and Simeon in the temple day by day, all those years, watching and waiting. Let us watch and wait here ourselves, perhaps just slowly repeating: 'We wait for your loving kindness, O God, in the midst of your temple.'

Then there was the child: already as an infant he had been incorporated into the community of faith by circumcision; now he was to be presented to God in the temple. But Mary and Joseph didn't stop there: he learned prayers and stories about God from his parents. On the cross he prayed a verse of a psalm he said as a child when he went to sleep: 'Into your hands I commend my spirit.' There would have been Sabbath meals every Friday with stories and rituals. He would have learned Hebrew in the synagogue's school. There would have been Sabbath worship in the synagogue. Later would have come his bar mitzvah, where he would have read a portion of Scripture in front of the congregation. What follow-up do Anglican children have after baptism? Or after confirmation? Or when they lead our choirs in churches and cathedrals? They say and sing a great deal, but is it interiorised as it is in the phrase from the Eucharist, 'feed on him in your hearts by faith with thanksgiving'? Let us spend a moment thinking of the rich religious education and training Jesus had and then let us pray for the religious training of our children.

'Let us all feed on him in our hearts by faith with thanksgiving.' The life of Jesus began with the shedding of blood in circumcision; his presentation in the temple begins with the shedding of blood in the sacrifice of the two birds. In the midst of this lovely and joyful occasion there is a stern warning to Mary: 'And a sword will pierce your own soul also.' I have always been amazed at Christians who lose their faith when suffering strikes them or strikes those they love. What is the sign we receive at baptism? The sign of the cross. Many make the sign of the cross as they worship. What is the central act of Christian worship Sunday after Sunday – the Eucharist at the heart of which is a narrative which begins: 'The Lord Jesus in the night that he was betrayed took bread.' Betrayal, suffering, cross. Dame Julian of Norwich said 'I was able to understand the compassion of our Lady St Mary. She and Christ were so one in their love that the greatness of her love caused the greatness of her suffering.'

Simeon's prayer, which is part of our liturgy at Evensong, begins: 'Lord now lettest thou thy servant depart in peace.' When I hear or say that I try to remember that I too will die, that I hope that Simeon's prayer will be sung or said as my coffin is carried out. I try to identify myself with the Glory be to the Father, Son and Holy Spirit that concludes Simeon's prayer: so much to be thankful for, so much to ask forgiveness for. When we die, we shall stand before God naked, with no pretences and no protection – we can't hide or deceive ourselves any more. I was reminded of that theme in an amusing way this last week. I was asked to lecture to a clerical dining club in London. I had sent on ahead a hand-out with the topic of my lecture and a reading list. When I arrived I discovered that it had not been photocopied. I produced my own copy of the hand-out on a rough piece of scrap paper with a page of my autobiography prepared for my grandchildren on the other side. Whoever then did the photocopying decided to copy both sides, meaning that the guests had a piece of sober academic work on the one side and on the other trivial but amusing stories of my boyhood. It was a parable: there was the front we present to the world on the one side; and on the other side there was what lies behind the public façade. There is a poignant poem by T.S. Eliot, 'A Song for Simeon', which contains the lines: 'My life is light, waiting for the death wind, / Like a feather on the back of my hand.' Simeon knew it was time to go: 'Lord now lettest thou thy servant depart in peace.' That will be true for us all one day.

We conclude by praying with St Augustine, in the final words of *The City of God* (XXII 30, 1091): 'There we shall be still and we shall see; we shall see and we shall love; we shall love and we shall praise. Behold what will be in the end without end! For what is our end but to reach that kingdom which has no end.'

# 10.

# A Pattern for Lent

Have you drawn up a pattern for Lent? A rule to govern your life? I recently read an article about a well-known MP. It described him as a 'keen Anglican' adding 'if that is not a contradiction in terms'. Perhaps the author was thinking of English Anglicans. As English Anglicans, we have been around for many centuries, linked to the monarchy and the powerful. Because of that, it is easy for us to lose our cutting edge, our distinctiveness. As St Paul wrote to the Christians in Rome: 'Conform no longer to the pattern of this present world.' (Romans 12:2.) Yet I think of the government of Zimbabwe, which refuses to allow Anglicans in and around Harare to use their church buildings. But the Anglicans there are not deterred by the absence of their church buildings. Instead they worship in the open air – and they do it enthusiastically. During Lent we examine ourselves and wonder whether we are allowing ourselves to be squeezed into the world's mould. Each year, Lent comes at the right time, just when we've become slack and there may be little to distinguish us from unbelievers. We've been squeezed into the ways and values of the world around us. You don't plan your holiday as you get onto the plane – you plan a holiday weeks ahead. If you haven't begun to plan Lent, it's a bit late, but not too late. Even if you have planned Lent, perhaps I may give you an opportunity to consider what you have planned against what I suggest. How are we going to use these precious six weeks to transform our lives?

What do you think about in the dentist's chair? I sometimes think about my next address, which you may think explains a lot. I was being treated at our marvellous Dental Academy. The final year student dentist was trying to work out whether the plate she had made would fit in my mouth. When it went in she said, 'Say Mississippi'. I said 'Mississippi'. 'Fabulous,' she replied. 'Now say it again.' I did so. 'Fantastic,' she said. I had been trying to think of a watchword I could give you this first Sunday of Lent. I quickly realised that Mississippi wouldn't do – four s's, four i's and two p's. Instead, I asked her where she came from. 'Epsom,' she replied. I thought that was just right and spent the rest of the time in the chair working out words for each letter of the word Epsom. These could be our guide, our pattern during Lent for Eucharist. There used to be an old slogan: 'The Lord's people at the Lord's service on the Lord's Day.' 'Do this,' said Jesus. If the early Christians had simply said their private prayers in their own homes, they would never have been arrested. Instead, from the beginning they met together to receive the risen Lord through the Scriptures and through bread and wine. In our own time, even in concentration camps, prisoners would scrounge a piece of bread, fill an enamel mug with water and celebrate the Eucharist – a sign of hope and love in a scene of death and despair. An ancient prayer expresses the longing of Christians throughout the centuries: 'Like as the watchman looks for the dawning of the day, so do we look for you O Christ. Come with the dawning of the day and make yourself known in scripture and the breaking of the bread for Prayer.'

A week or two ago the Saturday *Guardian* included a small booklet, 'How to Meditate, Ten Easy Steps'. Meditation is an OK word – one can't imagine a *Guardian* booklet called 'How to Pray, Ten Easy Steps'. Yet everything in the booklet is really about prayer posture, attention, silence, focussing on a phrase. Find ten minutes each day, the same time each day if at all possible so you don't forget. Then as the psalm says, 'Be still and know that I am God'. You could link up your own prayer with the prayer of the whole church by taking the Sunday liturgy sheet home and using it each day. Slowly pray the Collect on Mondays. Meditate on the Old Testament lesson on Tuesdays and turn it into prayer. Do the same with the psalm on Wednesdays and the epistle on Thursdays. On Fridays read the Gospel slowly and meditatively. On Saturdays pray and ponder the prayers at the offertory and after communion. In this way you keep up your friendship with God through the prayer of the body of Christ, the church. If we are to spend all eternity with God, hadn't we better get to know him now? Study. When did you last read anything about the Christian faith? You are on the front lines in the conflict with atheism, which is more confident than it has been for many generations. Are you well-equipped for the battle? The bookshop has Lent books as well as books on many other subjects. Why not join one of the Bible study groups? Or one of the Lent Groups?

Jesus has been called 'The Man for Others'. The Eucharist is a school of love – we wait for one another to go up, to kneel, we wait for the bread, we wait for the cup. We eat of the same bread; drink of the same cup. Have you ever said 'Hello' to that person you've knelt beside at the altar?

The Eucharist is about communion, community, sharing the common life. Do we look for Christ in the people we meet, the people we live with, the people we see in front of us in the Co-Op queue? Then there is the question of money. Oh, dear, why mention money? Because we are flesh and blood people who live in the material world and work with it. Christianity isn't a spiritual religion that rejects the material world. It's a sacramental religion that helps us use the material world to bring us to God. We think of the flesh and blood of Jesus, the sacraments using water, bread and wine, hands, and oil. Do we give away five or even ten per cent of our income after tax? Or is money an area of life we'd prefer to keep separated from God? Yet when we bring up bread and wine at the Eucharist we also offer up money. The bread and wine have been cultivated, processed, bought, and sold. They have been through the commercial process, delivered by transport, the subject of phone calls, invoices, and financial calculations. When we put bread and wine on the altar, we are placing on the altar all the commercial and physical processes which have enabled them to be there after a long journey.

I recommend that we go to Epsom for Lent: E for Eucharist, P for Prayer, S for Study, O for Other people, M for material possessions, including money. That will give us a framework for living Lent – and indeed for more Christian living throughout the year.

# 11.

# Lent: Desert and Ash

Lent can be a decisive, life changing turning point for all of us. Perhaps this Lent for the first time, you will promise to take daily prayer seriously, or make the Eucharist central to your Christian life, or make your first confession to God in the presence of a priest, or engage in some study with others, or say no to yourself in order to free yourself to say yes to God. As we keep Lent, I offer you two evocative images: desert and ash. I hope they speak to you as they speak to me.

## *Desert*

'The Spirit immediately drove Jesus out into the wilderness,' St Mark tells us at the beginning of his Gospel. The Jews had been led by God through the desert. The Jews were bounded by the desert to the south. With the wind in the right place, a family could wake up to discover fine sand in every crevice of their home. You could wake up almost tasting sand in your mouth. The desert is a place of tremendous contrasts, sweltering heat during the day, bitterly cold at night – as the refugees from Libya experience in their camps on the borders of Tunisia at the moment. The desert is a place where life is stripped down to essentials. Above all, it is a place of total silence. When the church became more worldly in the fourth century, some fled to the desert, and became known as the desert fathers and mothers. A traveller who was curious about these monks and nuns asked to see two of these well-known fathers. He was given a vision of them in two boats. In the first sat the Holy Spirit and one father in complete silence. In the second sat the other father with the angels of God. They were all eating honey cakes. When the former Archbishop of Canterbury, Rowan Williams, wrote his recent book about the wisdom of the desert, he called it *Silence and Honey Cakes*. Our often worldly church needs the desert; those who go off into communities in which silence is central to their lives. I try to go on retreat twice a year to communities like Alton Abbey near here: in the silence, everything and everyone looks different – an orange on the plate at breakfast, a bird pecking at the lawn, my own life.

By contrast, many think of faith as 'poor little talkative Christianity', like a despairing character in E.M. Forster's *A Passage to India*. During Lent, sit in a chair and be silent for ten minutes, using a phrase like 'Our Father' as you breathe in and out. You will find there is a presence at the heart of every silence. When someone comes to consult me, we often begin with a period of silence together. 'Silence somehow reaches to the heart of our human problem', wrote the Archbishop in his book. He commented on the spiritual dangers for ordained people, who have a licence to talk. Talkative people who arrived to speak to the desert fathers and mothers were often brought to a halt when the monks were silent or only uttered just one or two hesitant words. Here in the cathedral, we have a moment's silence after each lesson. Would it be a helpful idea to lengthen it gradually until we spent five minutes in silence, so we could mull over what we had heard? In church we often rush from one thing to another and never meditate on what we are saying or singing. The French poet Péguy published a long poem. When people bought the book they were angry to find that every few pages there was a blank page. Asked why he had included so many blank pages, he replied, 'To give you time to think.'

## *Ash*

'Dust you are and to dust you will return, repent and believe the Gospel.' We heard those words on Ash Wednesday when we received the sign of the cross in ashes on our foreheads. I always feel that it is like standing on the doorstep between heaven and earth. We would know that the church was really getting the Gospel across if people crowded in on Ash Wednesday as they do at Christmas. The basic truth about each one of us is summed up in three short statements: 'I am made by God. I am made for God. I am made to go to God.' We reach fifty or sixty and we realise that our most important choices in life have already been made: in education, marriage, children, or work. Yet even then we don't truly understand that like everyone else we shall become ash and dust. Other people die, but not me. There is a passage about transience in Eliot's poem 'Four Quartets':

> Ash on an old man's sleeve
> Is all the ash the dead roses leave.
> Dust in the air suspended

Marks the place where a story ended.
Dust inbreathed was a house
The wall, the wainscot and the mouse.

In the Buddhist tradition, the first noble truth is called *dukkha*. The word means that all life is imperfect and transitory, and includes all kinds of suffering, such as mental and physical. We try to dodge this, to pretend that it is not true. When we accept that it is true, however, there is a great liberation. This is particularly the case when we accept in heart and mind the fact that one day both your name and mine will be on the list of those to be prayed for at the Eucharist because we've died the previous week.

Pierre Teilhard de Chardin, who died in 1955, was a French Jesuit theologian and scientist. In one of his books he meditated on his own dying: 'O God, grant that I may understand that if is You . . . who are painfully parting the fibres of my being in order to penetrate to the very marrow of my substance and bear me away within Yourself.' When my parents died thirty years ago, we had to decide what to put on the stone where their ashes lay. I suggested 'Remembered before God'. I was wrong. I should have suggested 'Remembered by God'. Thirty years ago they were remembered by us and by many people in their village, but the time is coming when they will be remembered by no one. What really matters, and what really gives us hope, is that they and we will be remembered by God.

# 12.

# Lent: Paying Attention

Those who want to save their life will lose it, and those who lose their life for my sake, and for the sake of the Gospel, will save it.

*Mark 8:35*

I can still hear my teacher shouting: 'Wilkinson! Stop looking out of the window and pay attention.' *Pay attention.* How about adding that to your Lent rule? When we open our eyes as babies we think we are the centre of the world: it all exists for me; my mother exists solely for me. But I am not the centre of the world: God is. In Waitrose car park the other day, someone had left a trolley in a car space. You might expect to find self-centred sin in car parks of other supermarkets but not in Waitrose. But there it was: a nuisance, a danger to parking cars. It was a self-centred act. What has this to do with paying attention? The person who left an empty trolley in the car park was acting thoughtlessly, being lazy, neither thinking of others nor paying attention to their needs.

Simone Weil, the French Jewish mystic, wrote: 'Every time we really concentrate our attention, we destroy the evil in ourselves.' Jesus saw self-centredness ('those who want to save their lives') as a desperate desire to hoard one's life: the fear that if we give ourselves away we will have nothing left. This theme connects up with today's story of Abraham from Genesis 17 and St Paul in Romans 4. As it is put in Hebrews: 'By faith Abraham obeyed when he was called to set out for a place . . . and he set out not knowing where he was going.' (11:8.) Every new relationship we make is like Abraham setting out for an unknown country; perhaps this new relationship will be delightful or alarming or, perhaps, challenging, like the desert was for Jesus. I want all of us to think of learning to pay attention to God, to other people and to the created world.

## 1. *Attention to God*

Imagine someone coming to the Eucharist. They kneel to pray: 'O God, I hope I've brought my collection. I'm worried I didn't turn the gas off. I do hope the Mass setting isn't going to be too modern. I wonder who the preacher is. I do wish the kneelers were more comfortable, for Christ's sake, Amen.' That's a caricature, but it isn't too far from the truth of some of our prayers, is it? That person never really takes her worried eyes off herself, never reaches out to God, never pays attention to God. Perhaps instead you might read and ponder the lessons quietly and turn them into prayer: 'Lord give me faith so that I may bravely go out to unknown experiences like Abraham.' Or it may be that we will simply want to repeat again and again a phrase that will take us to God. 'Be still and know that I am God.' When we try to do that, our attention wanders. It may be we have to spend our time just gently bringing our attention back to God through the phrase: 'Be still and know that I am God.'

A study showed that people spend fifty per cent of their time doing one thing and thinking of another subject. It's not surprising that trying to pay attention to God can be difficult. We might reflect that we ought to be preparing to attend to God here in this life. There won't be much else to do in heaven but to attend to God. How do we react to that prospect?

## 2. *Paying Attention to People*

Imagine walking down the High Street preoccupied with some worry, some concern, some memory, some fear. As a result, you don't pay attention to anyone whom you pass. Paying attention means being fully present in each situation, and often we aren't. By contrast there is the Christian concept of 'The Sacrament of the Present Moment'. Buddhists speak of 'Mindfulness', which is the same idea under a different name. When I began my training for the priesthood at Mirfield, each student was given one of the monks as a spiritual director. Some of us were given Fr Trevor Huddleston. After years of fighting for the rights of black people in South Africa, he had returned to the Mother House of the Community of the Resurrection. He was world famous. When I went to see him for the first time, he didn't start talking about himself but instead focussed totally on me. I felt valued and listened to as a unique individual, not as just another student.

How easy it is not to attend to people, not really to look at them, not really to listen, not really to take an interest! This is a temptation not just with strangers, but also with those who are close to us. How familiar is this type of dialogue? 'Darling, did you hear what I said?' 'No, what did you say?' 'You aren't really here, are you? Are you thinking of your next sermon?' Attend to God, attend to people.

## 3. Attend to the Created World

'Have you seen the daffodils in the garden?' 'No, I didn't look.' Ruskin, the Victorian art critic, used to say to his students that he wasn't teaching them to draw. Rather, he was teaching them to see. For Stanley Spencer, the twentieth-century British artist, everything was fascinating. If you go to his chapel near Newbury, you will see his murals depicting his experiences of the First World War. Over the altar is a general resurrection of soldiers killed in the war, but to reach it you have to go by way of ordinary military life: horses, hospital beds being made, ambulances, maps, stretchers and a hot water bottle. He described Cookham on Thames, where he lived, as possessed by a sacred presence of which the inhabitants were not aware. Echoing Moses (Genesis 3), he remarked, 'I saw many burning bushes in Cookham.' In Spencer's paintings, Jesus preaches to people at the Regatta, he holds the Last Supper in the Oast House, he carries his cross through the main streets, and the resurrection takes place in the churchyard. One of Spencer's pictures includes old bicycle wheels, a bucket with a hole, a rusty grate, and drainpipes. He paid attention to everything, especially the ugly and unimportant. Jesus paid attention to ordinary things – fields, mustard water, seeds, trees, pigs, mountains, and the lake. On the night he was betrayed he also paid attention to ordinary things, to bread and wine. That is why we are here.

Someone I knew was very depressed and sat in the garden in despair, blind to the sunshine, blind to all the love which surrounded him; totally absorbed by his own misery. But one day, for a moment, his attention was diverted by a small bird trying to pull a thread out of an old rag for its nest. For the first time for months he was totally absorbed by something outside himself. By paying attention to something outside himself he began to recover. He stopped clinging onto himself and by losing himself found himself. This Lent, attend to God, attend to other people and attend to the world. If you lose yourself, you will find yourself.

# 13.

# Lent: Dying to Live

From today's Epistle, I Corinthians 1:23-4: 'We proclaim Christ crucified . . . Christ the power of God and the wisdom of God.' The cross has a universal message, a universal meaning, a universal application, a universal image. We discover the cross in the most unexpected places, as I did when I recently recorded a late night film, *Life as a House*. It was only a minor film and I confess I was only attracted to it because Kristin Scott Thomas starred in it.

*Life as a House* is about George, a man in his fifties who works in an architect's office. He makes models of proposed buildings but after twenty years he has still not got round to rebuilding the shack where he lives. The management decides that the advent of computer modelling has made his work unnecessary, so he is declared redundant. He stumbles out of the building in a rage and collapses outside, where he is taken to hospital. Tests show he has cancer and has only four months to live. He decides he is going to use the remaining months of his life to mend his relationships and turn the shack where he lives into a proper house.

George's teenage son, Sam, lives with his ex-wife and her new husband. Sam is in fierce rebellion against the adult world – he takes drugs, plays ear-splitting music, looks like a Gothic vampire with his face and ears pierced with studs and rings. After many battles, his father persuades Sam to live with him for the summer and gets him to help with the rebuilding of the house. Gradually, after many rows, Sam and his father begin to understand one another and even begin love one another as they had done years ago, when Sam was a little boy and the apple of his father's eye. As they work on the house, Sam asks his father 'How do you become something you are not?' and his father explains that this happens when you allow yourself to be loved. George's ex-wife is grateful beyond measure that he has managed to make a good relationship with their son. She regularly comes round and sees the demolition of the shack and the rebuilding of the new house. She and George also begin to forgive one another and to heal old wounds. By the time George dies, the shack has been rebuilt into a pleasant house, his son has been healed of his addictions, self-hatred and isolation, and is reconciled with his father and mother, and George and his former wife have forgiven one another for the past.

The critic in the paper described the film as a tear-jerker; it was certainly over-simplified, for we all know that broken relationships rarely heal so smoothly or so quickly. Nevertheless, it was a moving and arresting parable for Lent and Holy Week. Why? Because the film began and ended with the impact of death on a family group. It began with George's realisation that he was going to die. This shocked him into repentance – in this case, the attempt to heal his broken relationships. The shack symbolised the wreck of his life. His demolition of it was an act of repentance; a turning around. Building a new home was a gesture of hope for a future that he would not be able to share. The whole film is about George's realisation that in order to get ready for his physical death, the old patterns of his life and relationships must die first so that he and those around him could live a new risen life.

When Lent began on Ash Wednesday, we received the sign of the cross in ashes on our foreheads and heard the words addressed to each one of us: 'Remember that you are dust and to dust you shall return; repent and believe the Gospel.' Lent begins with a reminder of our mortality, a reminder of our deaths, that we shall return to dust and ashes: and in the light of this we are urged to repent, to turn around. Each day in Lent in the liturgy we have reminders that we are moving towards Good Friday and the death of Christ. We can't get to Easter Day and resurrection without dying throughout Lent and on Good Friday.

Let us ponder today's three lessons, which are like a triptych. In the centre is the Epistle itself, with St Paul writing about the cross: 'we proclaim Christ crucified . . . Christ the power of God and the wisdom of God'. On the left panel are the Ten Commandments from the Old Testament (Exodus 20:1-17). Through the Ten Commandments, God can still speak to us about dying to self-centredness and rising to a new sense of our love for God and neighbour in society. What idols do I worship? What place has the sabbath in my life – are there times when I give my attention wholly to God and give up my frantic busyness? What do I covet?

Finally, on the right hand panel there is the Gospel story from St John (2:13-22). It tells how Jesus drove the traders out of the temple. In St Matthew's version of the story, Jesus says: 'My house shall be a house of prayer, but you have made it a den of robbers.' (21:13.) What goes on in our inner temples as well as in our churches – are we, are they houses of prayer, houses devoted to attention to God, love for God? Love for people in need? On Good Friday, where was the real temple situated? The real temple was not found in all its splendour at the centre of Jerusalem, but outside the gates.

There is the true worship: a young man on a cross struggling with all that is thrown against him, battling on so he can offer his life and prayer to his Father. As he said at the end of the battle: 'Father, into your hands I commend my spirit' (Luke 23:46). In the film, George realised that his old way of life must die before he would be ready to die himself. The altar to which we shall come in a few minutes is a place of sacrifice, a place of dying, a place of surrender.

'Lord forgive what we have been; sanctify what we are; guide what we shall become, for your glory. Amen.'

# 14.

# Holy Week: Maundy Thursday

The Lord Jesus on the night when he was betrayed, took a loaf of bread, and when he had given thanks, he broke it, and said 'This is my body that is for you. Do this in remembrance of me . . .' he took the cup also, after supper, saying, 'This cup is the new covenant in my blood. Do this, as often as you drink it, in remembrance of me.'

*I Corinthians 11:23-5*

When the forces of evil were gathering for their final assault, Jesus gave thanks. When hatred and fear were rising hour by hour in the hearts of the people, Jesus gave thanks. In the midst of the disciples who were even then squabbling as to who was the greatest among them, he gave thanks. In the presence of Judas he gave thanks. Among disciples who were soon to desert him he gave thanks. He used words very like those we use today when bread and wine are brought to our altars: 'Blessed be thou O Lord our God, eternal king who bringest forth bread from the earth. Blessed be thou O Lord God, eternal king who createst the fruit of the vine.' We would expect a man facing torture and execution to be preoccupied with himself, his terrors and regrets, his rage and his resentments. Perhaps he might be numb and paralysed; a frozen, helpless victim. But Jesus, on the night when his friend betrayed him and the rest deserted him, was not consumed with resentment nor paralysed by fear: he moved out from his own centre to the things on the table in front of him in gratitude, and gave thanks for them and for what lay ahead. He did this so that he and they may be consecrated in sacrifice for others to the glory of God. 'This is my body which is broken for you.' 'This is my blood which is shed for you.' He must have been at ease with his own body to be able to say that.

Day by day throughout his whole life he has given himself away for the sake of God and other people. Now that life of daily self-sacrifice is reaching its final expression. Now more than ever he struggles every inch of the way to turn the worst that people can hurl at him into an act of offering, even an act of worship, for his Father. After supper, he takes the humble role of the servant and washes the feet of the disciples – those parts of our body which we prefer to keep hidden, our feet with their calluses and bunions and comically shaped toes. Then he goes into the Garden, where he struggles with the temptation to run away; then he is mocked and beaten up by soldiers; then the crucifixion itself. At each stage he struggles to make it an offering and act of worship: my body given for you; my life blood given for you. This has been so at every Eucharist since: that extraordinary self-giving, where Jesus gives himself to devout and careless alike. See the variety of hands outstretched – young, smooth hands, manicured hands, arthritic hands, hands roughened by hard manual work. Hands from every stage of life. Christ given for her, for him, for my friend, for my enemy, for the person I dislike, for the person I ignore, for the person I love best in the world. Bishop Gore called the Eucharist the sacrament of fraternity for a reason.

So tonight before we go, in order to share something of the darkness and struggle of Jesus in Gethsemane, we pause to share his company in the brightly lit upper room. He takes bread and wine. This is my body broken for you. This is my blood which is shed for you. And he takes our feet into his hands and washes them.

# 15.

# Good Friday According to St Mark

We are going to listen to and ponder four different accounts of the crucifixion. They were written by four Gospel writers for four different Christian communities. Each Gospel communicates the faith of its writer, but also the faith of the community out of which it emerged. These early Christians were asking not only for the story of the crucifixion to be preserved so it could be passed on to future generations, they were asking 'What did the story mean? How should we understand it and communicate it to others? Will we also be sent to our deaths?'

The Gospel of Mark was completed about 65 CE but the narrative of passion was probably written earlier, perhaps within ten years of the crucifixion itself, and probably written for the Christian community in Rome. It may well have been written to be recited at Easter Eucharist celebrating Christ's death and resurrection. At this Eucharist new Christians would be baptised, would die and rise with Christ. That wasn't just talk. They might be arrested as they left their meeting place and then be tried and put to death.

Mark's Gospel was composed for Christians who had a strong sense of the dark side of life, for those who were going through times when they felt abandoned by God. It is not for those who seem always to walk on the sunny side of the street. Here is God revealed in a powerless captive under sentence of death all alone, with everyone, even his followers, ranged against him. He goes to a death reserved for only slaves and the worst criminals. This is not God as a huggable daddy who will make everything all right. The motif is neither the heroism of Jesus nor horror at his sufferings. Rather, the story focuses on how evil does its worst, yet God uses even evil for his own purposes. In Mark, Jesus goes to his death utterly alone. From the end of the Last Supper Jesus is isolated. The disciples sleep in the Garden, desert him when he is arrested and Peter denies him. 'Darkness came over the whole land. . . . Jesus cried out with a loud voice 'Eloi, Eloi, lema sabacthani?' . . . 'My God, my God, why have you forsaken me?' (Mark 15:33-4.)

As Jesus battled against evil, he went down into the worst and darkest part of human experience: the sense of being abandoned by God. The words of Psalm 22 come to him: one of the psalms in which the righteous man, persecuted and reviled, calls upon the apparently absent and indifferent God. The prayer of protest is one of the most real forms of prayer. Psalm 22 liked a dark road with occasional points of light. What stock of scripture can you draw upon when you are in despair? A woman once came up to me after a funeral and told me that her two grown-up children had died during the last year. 'I'm off God at the moment.' My God, my God, why? Jesus enters into the experience of those who still call upon God even though they receive only silence and darkness. All true faith includes times of struggle and doubt. A theologian was struck by blindness in his forties. All his books and typed notes were now useless to him, but he reassessed his terrible gift and with it came the grace to bear his darkness on behalf of all the disabled. He wrote a book he called *In the Beginning was Darkness*, because creation starts in darkness.

> When the centurion, who stood facing him, saw that in this way
> Jesus breathed his last, he said 'Truly this man was God's Son!'
>
> *Mark 15:39*

What did the centurion mean by this? Romans believed in many gods. But what matters is what those early Christians in Rome believed – some of whom, like the centurion, were not Jews but Romans or Gentiles. They had responded to the cross by choosing to be baptised. They had come to believe that this outcast on the rubbish heaps outside the civilised city had opened a new way to God. The veil in the temple was torn apart so that the sacred place was no longer concealed.

A French bishop once told the story of how once on a Saturday night a group of boys were at a loose end. One of them volunteered to go into the church. As a joke, he confessed the worst sins he could think of to the priest. When the boy finished the priest said 'Go and kneel in front of that crucifix and say, deliberately and slowly, "I know you died for me, and I don't care a damn."' The bishop said, 'I know that the story is true, because I was that boy.'

# 16.
# Good Friday According to St Luke

Alan and Verity were told from the beginning that their baby Christopher, their first child, would not live long. He died when he was six months old. During his brief life and after his death, his parents struggled to understand why a child born in the image of God should be so disabled. Eventually they came to believe, as they wrote, 'Christopher was the Good Friday image of God, the weakness, the broken-body image. . . . He did not grow himself but he helped other people to grow both spiritually and emotionally. . . . He allowed us to discover depths of love we didn't know we had.'

St Luke, a Greek doctor, wrote his Gospel in about 75 CE, some ten years after Mark. He addressed both his Gospel and Acts to a high ranking Roman civil servant. Luke wanted to attract as wide a range of people as possible. It was written from within the faith of a Christian community, possibly one in Syria. He presents Jesus as particularly concerned for those who don't belong; the people on the edges of society.

> Jesus said 'Father, forgive them, for they do not know what they are doing'.
>
> *Luke 23:34*

For Luke, Jesus is the one who befriended the people rejected by society and religion. Only Luke tells us that the shepherds were the first to greet the child Jesus – shepherds were regarded as an irreligious lot. Only Luke tells us the parables of the prodigal son and the Good Samaritan. Only Luke tells us that from the cross Jesus pardoned the penitent criminal. 'Father, forgive them.' We are so used to hearing this saying that we forget how extraordinary it was, and still is. Our natural reaction to hatred, scorn and violence is to retaliate. There are families, relationships and marriages which daily enact the kind of constant retaliation we see between Palestinians and Israelis. There needs to be someone or some group who stops the cycle of retaliation by absorbing the violence.

But Jesus' forgiveness did not prevent him from being crucified. His forgiveness did not convert the soldiers. Instead, he pioneered a different way; following his example, Stephen, the first martyr, forgave his persecutors as he died. The readiness of Nelson Mandela to forgive those who had imprisoned him gave South Africa a new start. The process continued with the Truth and Reconciliation Commission under Archbishop Tutu, which enabled people to confess to their crimes before their victims. 'Father, forgive them.' Forgiveness is often long-term work, even a lifetime's work. For it involves constantly replacing the desire for hatred and retaliation with compassion and forgiveness. Are our own lives spoiled by failures to forgive?

> The leaders scoffed at him, saying, 'He saved others; let him save himself if he is the Messiah.'
>
> *Luke 23:35*

Suppose Jesus had run away from the Garden and saved his own skin? Say he had lived another thirty years and died in his bed. He could never have said, 'I lay down my life for the sheep' (John 10:15). The cross was the climax to a life of self-giving, the sacrifice which crowned his sacrifices day in day out. We experience this generous self-giving of Jesus at every Eucharist. There are mediaeval pictures showing God the Father holding the cross with infinite compassion while the Holy Spirit streams from Father to Son. 'You cannot save yourself,' they taunted Jesus. The self-giving Jesus is the self-giving of God, Father, Son and Spirit.

The theologian Bill Vanstone, whose hymn 'Morning Glory' we sing, described how a surgeon once carried out a particular brain operation which had never before been attempted. It involved seven hours continuous attention and self-giving. At the end he was led out of the operating theatre blind with fatigue. Such is the self-giving of God, spent and drained in the self-giving that created and which sustains the universe. The self-giving of Jesus on the cross is in the image of the self-giving love of God.

> Jesus, crying with a loud voice, said: 'Father, into your hands I commend my spirit.'
>
> *Luke 23:46*

The last cry in Mark is a cry of desolation. The last cry in Luke is one of confident trust. It comes from Psalm 31. He had learned it as a childhood prayer before going to sleep. When Terry Waite was a hostage, chained to a radiator for years, he prayed parts of the Prayer Book he remembered from his days as a choirboy. A man dying after many months of suffering from dementia suddenly sat up and recited the whole of Psalm 23, then lay down and died. What spiritual resources have we to draw upon in times of sickness and distress? 'Father, into your hands I commend my spirit.' Throughout life there are many occasions when we have to let go with as much confident trust as we can muster – leaving home for the first time, when in turn our children leave home, when we retire, when we are conscious of ageing and having to let others do what we had enjoyed doing, and finally in the last stages of dying. Those who are able to let go and commit themselves to God at each stage experience resurrection and new life.

# 17.

# Good Friday According to St Matthew

In 85 CE, perhaps twenty years after St Mark's Gospel was completed, St Matthew writes his own Gospel. If Luke (around 75 CE) wrote as a Greek, Matthew writes very much as a Jewish Christian. Perhaps he also wrote for Gentiles; he certainly revised and added to Mark. But the purpose of all four Gospels was always the purpose expressed by St John: 'These are written so that you may come to believe that Jesus is the Messiah, the Son of God, and that through believing you may have life in his name.' (20:31.)

> They offered him wine to drink, mingled with gall; but when he had tasted it, he would not drink it.
>
> *Matthew 27:34*

Compassionate women used to offer a drink to those about to be crucified that would dull the pain. Jesus is offered the drink but refuses to drink it. Why? Because Jesus had work to do and he wanted to be as clear-headed as possible. Work? What was that work? He was battling to keep the channel open in himself between humanity and God.

A few years ago, there was a ferry disaster. As the boat was sinking, a courageous man stretched himself across a huge gap and people crawled to safety across his body. Jesus was like a human bridge stretched across a chasm. The earliest hymns about the Passion from the sixth century picture Jesus as a warrior against the forces of evil: 'Sing my tongue the glorious battle'; 'The royal banners forward go'. Jesus took the worst evil could throw at him and battled to turn it into an act of obedience, love and worship offered to God. This is atonement: uniting humanity and God at one in himself at great cost. It was necessary for him to suffer not to placate an angry God, not to fulfil Scripture, but because of who Jesus was and who we are.

The way Jesus lived and loved was bound to come into conflict with us selfish, cruel and vindictive human beings. When we become united with him in baptism, Eucharist and prayer, his life begins to flow into ours. As we cooperate with him so he begins to create in us a revulsion against anything which separates us from him. That is how he takes away the sin of the world.

Two bandits were crucified with him.

*Matthew 27:38*

You can tell a man by the company he keeps. Where would you find Jesus on most days of his life and here on Good Friday? Among the rejected; the people beyond the pale. St Martin-in-the-Fields in central London has had a ministry to the homeless and down and outs since the First World War. When I preached there a few years ago I was glad to see that tramps were asleep in some of the back pews. Downstairs, the church was providing advice and food. For Jesus there was no 'us' and 'them', no club for insiders from which you could look out with superiority and pity on the rest of the world. In the end, he hung between two guerrillas. You can tell a man by the company he keeps.

The earth shook and the rocks were split. The tombs also were opened, and many bodies of the saints who had fallen asleep were raised.

*Matthew 27:51-2*

This story is only found in Matthew, who was keen on portents, earthquakes and visions. Early Christians asked 'What about people who lived before Jesus, what about our ancestors? Will they share in the fruits of Christ's work too?' Matthew answers this question by telling this story. A passage in 1 Peter (3:19) answers the same question with a picture of Jesus going to preach to the spirits of the dead to tell them the good news. These stories express the same truth we hear on Easter Eve in the blessing of the great Easter Candle: 'Christ yesterday and today; the beginning and the end; Alpha and Omega. His are all times and all ages. To him be glory and dominion through the ages of eternity. Amen.'

# 18.

# Good Friday According to St John

In this fourth meditation we move to St John's Gospel. It has a very different atmosphere from that of the first three Gospels, Mark, Luke and Matthew. John was written about 90 CE, thirty years or more after Mark. Jesus here is a more majestic figure, even at times more distant than in the first three Gospels. John's account of the crucifixion omits all the horror and struggle. He omits the story of the Garden of Gethsemane with its agony and temptations. Instead, as Jesus goes to the cross he says to his disciples, 'Courage, the victory is mine.' Jesus is always in control. By quoting Scripture John was asserting that even though events seem to deny God, he was nevertheless working out his purposes.

> So they took Jesus and carrying the cross by himself, he went out to what is called The Place of the Skull, which in Hebrew is called Golgotha.
>
> *John 19:16-17*

Whereas in the other three Gospels Simon of Cyrene carries the cross at least part of the way, John tells us that Jesus carried the cross by himself. John wishes to emphasise that Jesus had the spiritual and physical strength necessary to carry the cross alone. John, even more than the other Gospels, sees the stories of Jesus in the light of the resurrection, which casts its victorious light back over the whole story. The earliest crucifixes depicted Jesus reigning as a king from the cross. It was only in the twelfth century, under the influence of the Franciscans, that crucifixes began to show him in agony. It was they who also invented the Christmas crib. They wanted to underline the truly human aspect to Jesus.

When Eastern Orthodox Christians depict the crucifixion they keep to the style of the early church. In the 1940s Graham Sutherland painted his famous and horrifyingly realistic crucifixion for St Matthew's Church in Northampton. Some Eastern Orthodox Christians visited the church, saw the picture and turned away, appalled. This painting did not portray the cross as a triumph in the light of the resurrection. This picture owed more to St Mark's account.

> Standing near the cross were his mother, and his mother's sister, Mary the wife of Clopas and Mary Magdalene. When Jesus saw his mother and the disciple whom he loved standing beside her, he said to his mother, 'Woman, here is your son.' Then he said to the disciple, 'Here is your mother.' And from that hour the disciple took her into his own home.
>
> *John 19:25-7*

Women played an important part in the ministry of Jesus. A group of women went with him on his tours with the twelve disciples. Women were the first people at the tomb on Easter Day. It was Mary Magdalene who told the disciples the news of the resurrection. When the Apostles gathered to await the coming of the Spirit at Pentecost, with them were various women, at the centre of whom was Mary, mother of Jesus.

On the cross Jesus continues his ministry of forgiveness and reconciliation. He creates a home in which Mary and John will care for one another. 'Woman' sounds rude, but in Judaism it was a formal mode of address for solemn occasions. Mary loses a son but gains a new one, John. He is the one who knows most fully the mind of her son, whom she is about to lose. Did she think of how Simeon's prophecy all those years ago in the temple was coming true? Did Mary remember his words, 'A sword will pierce your own soul too'? Mary also had known rejection, so she was united with her son in his agony of being despised and rejected. Here Mary becomes mother of all believers. She was the mother who gave a body to her son, and now she becomes the mother of the new body of Christ, the church. Jesus says to us all, 'Here is your mother'.

In Rome recently, I once again visited St Peter's Basilica with its grandiose colonnade. It all seemed to speak more of power than love. But there was a statue there inside St Peter's that spoke more of love than power – Michelangelo's *Pietà*, where Mary cradles her dead son in her arms with infinite love and compassion.

> It is finished.
>
> *John 19:30*

It is done, it is completed. This word from the cross sums up John's understanding of the cross as victory. Even in his dying moments, Jesus is actively offering it all to his Father. 'He gave up his spirit' means that he handed it over. If we read on a few verses, we discover that a soldier thrust a spear into Jesus' side to make sure he was dead. Water and blood flowed out. For John this symbolised baptism and the Eucharist. What Jesus finished is continued in the life of the church. That is why we are here this Good Friday.

# 19.

# Easter: Seeing and Believing

Blessed are those who have not seen, yet have come to believe.

*John 20:29*

The section about the resurrection in St John's Gospel is very different from the earlier chapters. Before the story of the crucifixion there are some seventeen chapters. They often consist almost entirely of long abstract passages which John has created out of the teachings and impact of Jesus. Some are accompanied by arguments between Jesus and the people. Then, suddenly, after the resurrection, we move into a much simpler world. There is no lengthy teaching, no long discourses, no arguments; it is all very vivid and homely, like the story in chapter 21 of Jesus cooking a fish breakfast for his disciples, who were worn out after a night's fishing. They had caught nothing. But the unexpected meeting with Jesus and a breakfast cooked by him was their experience of a resurrection indeed, new life after a dark night. Today's Gospel passage from John 20:19-31 falls into two main sections. The first is when Jesus appears to his disciples after the resurrection.

> On the evening of that first day of the week, when the disciples were together, with the doors locked for fear of the Jewish leaders, Jesus came and stood among them and said, 'Peace be with you!' After he said this, he showed them his hands and side.
>
> *John 20:19-20*

The setting is on the first Easter Sunday in the evening. The disciples have barricaded themselves in. They are determined that they are not going to go the way of Jesus. They want to be safe. They want to protect themselves from suffering and death. But Jesus appears, shows them his hands and wounded side. Then he tells them to do the very thing they were determined not to do. They have to unlock those doors and go out into the world that crucified him. 'As the Father has sent me, so I send you.' (20:21.) He gives them the Holy Spirit and the command to continue his ministry of forgiveness. 'If you forgive the sins of any, they are forgiven.'

Jesus is clear: his ministry is not over. It is just beginning. He will minister through them; through his new body, the church. Wherever the church continues Christ's ministry it brings his forgiveness, as it has done in South Africa. During the Cold War, I saw the Conference of European Churches bring Eastern and Western Christians together. Christ's forgiving ministry is vivid in the sacramental ministry of confession. Every priest at ordination is commissioned to convey God's forgiveness. I remember a psychiatrist saying that every patient he treated was sick through lack of forgiveness – unable to forgive life, their parents, or themselves.

The second important section comes shortly after the first:

> Now Thomas (also known as Didymus), one of the Twelve, was not with the disciples when Jesus came. So the other disciples told him, 'We have seen the Lord!'
> But he said to them, 'Unless I see the nail marks in his hands and put my finger where the nails were, and put my hand into his side, I will not believe.'

Thomas was not there for the resurrection. Thomas is clear. Until he sees the nail marks in the hands of Jesus and puts his finger into the wounds in his hands and side, he cannot believe. By the time St John's Gospel was written in 90 CE or so, many of the original eyewitnesses had died. A new generation was being baptised which had never seen Jesus. Some were like one of my children who, after prayers, looked up and said, 'If only I could see Jesus.' But John knew that seeing did not inevitably lead to believing. Many had seen Jesus in his lifetime and did not come to belief, so Jesus says, 'Blessed are those who have not seen, yet have come to believe.'

Many of the original readers of St John's Gospel were in the same boat as us. How do we come to believe when we have not seen? Many come to believe in the same way as those two disciples did on their way to Emmaus. Their hearts burned within them while Jesus expounded the Scriptures; and he was revealed to them in the breaking of bread (Luke 24). We recognise how this was a pattern for the Eucharist which we still follow this morning: Jesus known through the word and the sacrament.

Anthony Bloom was for many years the Russian Archbishop in London. After the Russian Revolution his family fled to Paris. He trained as a doctor; he was a determined atheist. But one day a friend persuaded him to hear a talk by a priest. He was repelled by what he heard and rushed home to check the talk against one of the Gospels. He chose the shortest, St Mark, because he didn't want to waste time on a longer text. While he was reading St Mark's Gospel, he became aware of a presence and realised it was Jesus – a presence he said later that had never left him. In the 1920s, 1900 years after that scene in the upper room, Jesus could still appear and call a young Russian doctor in Paris to follow him and continue his ministry. 'Blessed are those who have not seen and yet have come to believe.'

We forget how extraordinary it is that suddenly, out of the blue, there appeared these twenty-seven documents that were later formed into what we call the New Testament. All these documents grew out of the faith of this new community after and through the resurrection. No person in ancient history is so well-documented by so many different pieces of writing as Jesus. Central to all of them is the resurrection. People since Christ have come to know him through the Scriptures and the Eucharist, the breaking of bread. 'Blessed are those who have not seen and yet have come to believe.'

Many people come to believe through contact with the believing community. The church has had a glorious record as well as a terrible one. We hear so much about the evils of religion that we forget its riches – treasures, as Paul put it, but treasures in earthen vessels (2 Corinthians 4:7).

When in 1968 Tony Bridge became Dean of Guildford people were fascinated to discover that for many years previously, he had been an atheist and painter. First of all, he had explored theology. He wrote in *They Became Christians*: 'I was appalled by the depth and profundity of Christian thinking, and by the cogency of the Gospel and the claims of Christ; for the very last thing I wanted to do was to become a Christian.' He was initially reluctant to join a Christian group, but that played a crucial part in his conversion: 'It was something in the group of people themselves: something about their quality of being, which left me feeling like a thirsty man in the desert who has suddenly been given a glimpse of a well-watered oasis. There was a lovingness, a peacefulness, a sense of shared and accepted purpose, a humbleness before facts which made me feel singularly small and lost.' Would an atheist visiting your home here in Portsmouth find a group of that character through this cathedral?

St John makes clear that in writing his Gospel he is not imparting neutral information like a timetable of the daily trains from Portsmouth Harbour to London Kings Cross. Instead, he says: 'These are written so that you may come to believe that Jesus is the Messiah, the Son of God, and that through believing you may have life in his name.' (John 20:31.)

# 20.
# Easter: The Resurrection of the Body

*I believe in the resurrection of the body, and the life everlasting.*

What do you make of these statements from the Apostles' Creed? This is an important theme for Eastertide. A priest friend of ours is eighty this month. He has served in the London area for his whole ministry. The Bishop of London's wife asked him, 'Would you like a party?' 'No, thank you, that's very kind,' he said. 'I'd prefer a performance of *The Dream of Gerontius*.' This was a surprising reply from a priest known for his radical views. On Thursday we will go to St Paul's Cathedral to see *The Dream of Gerontius*. Gerontius means 'old man' in Greek. Newman's text and Elgar's noble music tell the story of the dying and death of an old man and his experiences as he moves towards the vision of God. It includes what has become the well-known hymn 'Praise to the holiest in the height'.

*The Dream of Gerontius* is not very popular today because Gerontius, faced with the prospect of appearing before God, feels an overwhelming sense of awe and, indeed, some fear. It's all very different from the casual attitude to death in the popular poems people insert in the *Evening News* or compose for plaques on park benches. There is an inscription on a bench near here facing the sea, 'Rest well, Rob. We'll be with you in no time.' Isn't that a bit presumptuous? Doesn't it imply that heaven is there for the asking? Doesn't it also imply that heaven is just a grand reunion of friends with such relations as we choose to invite? But what is heaven unless it is a union with God, a return to God?

I hope that when we are dying we will all ask for the last rites of penitence, anointing and communion. This is known as the 'viaticum'. That is a significant term, meaning 'provisions for a journey'. What sort of journey? However, many people today, including, alas, some Christians, believe that death is the end. If there's no heaven then there's no journey. 'Always remembered', it says on many graves. But what happens when all the mourners have died? The really crucial question is whether God goes on remembering us.

The Jews took a long time to develop a belief in a life after death. For most of the Old Testament there are only a few vague hints of this kind of belief. They did not believe in the immortal soul. They could not envisage a life without a body. When a belief in life after death emerged in the books written between the testaments, it was expressed in terms of resurrection: a transformed new life for the whole person, not just for a soul, or spirit. This new belief in life after death, in resurrection, arose out of the fundamental belief that God in this life offers a relationship to human beings.

In Psalm 73, the psalmist wrote: 'Whom have I in heaven but thee: and there is none upon earth that I desire in comparison of thee.' The growing belief in a life after death was rooted in the Jewish longing for a continuation of that rich relationship with God: 'Like as the hart desireth the waterbrooks: so longeth my soul after thee, O God.' (Psalm 42.) Moreover, the Jewish experience of exile and restoration provided experiences of resurrection, of a new life after a type of death. When Jews returned from exile they knew God had resurrected a community which had been scattered and destroyed, hence Ezekiel's vision of the dry bones of the nation during the exile (Ezekiel 37). He expressed the Jewish longing for God to come and to breathe new life into the nation. We heard in the first lesson that after exile came the restoration, the resurrection of the temple: 'The latter splendour of this house shall be greater than the former, says the Lord of hosts.' (Haggai 2:9.)

The new Coventry Cathedral was consecrated in 1962 alongside the empty shell of the old one, which had been bombed. At the consecration service, the lesson was the one we heard tonight from Haggai. The Archbishop of Canterbury preached on that text: 'The latter splendour of this house shall be greater than the former, says the Lord of hosts.' First of all, therefore, a Christian belief in life after death should derive from our relationship with God. My old Professor of English in Cambridge was a devout Methodist. In a lecture about life after death, he confessed that when he felt reluctant to pray, he told himself: 'You'd better get used to God's company. Soon you'll have no other.' Some young people deride marriage as boring; always the same person all the time, year after year. But a few years pass and that young person meets someone whom he grows to love. He then says excitedly, 'I'm getting married.' What has changed? It is no longer marriage in the abstract, as a concept, but marriage with a beloved person. That makes all the difference. If we can say, at least at times, that we long for God, then we are getting ready for heaven; then heaven makes sense. Are we aimless wanderers or pilgrims with a goal in mind?

Jehovah's Witnesses will tell you that only a hundred and forty-four thousand people will be saved, but as the Church of England report *The Mystery of Salvation* stated in 1995, 'It is incompatible with the essential Christian affirmation that God is love to say that God brings millions into the world to damn them' (180). We can trust that those who have never had the chance to respond to God's love will have an opportunity to do so beyond the grave. We can trust that those who died as infants or who were crippled by mental disability will have the opportunity for growth and healing beyond the grave. We can trust that we will discover that different routes lead to the one God. Will there be any in the end who refuse God's offer? Are there those who are so given to evil that they cannot respond? We cannot tell. But we should always remind ourselves of the solemn responsibility of having the freedom to choose. Our choices have eternal consequences. 'No one can be compulsorily installed in heaven,' says the report (198). It adds that hell is not eternal torment but the final choosing of that which is opposed to God. Those who choose against God cease to be. When we go to a doctor, we want his diagnosis, his judgement, his truth. We ask the same from God. This indeed is awesome.

Paul in the second lesson (I Corinthians 3:12-13) writes that when anyone builds a house, the quality of the building work would be revealed if it caught fire. Some people disbelieve in heaven, not because it is incredible but because it is alarming. The Scriptures, prayer and sacraments remind us that we are made for better things. 'I am made by God. I am made for God. I have made to go to God.' Do we believe in the possibility of transformation? A cartoon depicted two caterpillars looking up at a butterfly. One says to the other, 'You'll never get me going up in one of those new contraptions.' To choose another image, we have been given the opportunity to soar away over the mountains like eagles; do we prefer to peck among the scraps like chickens? What if we are made to be eagles? God in this life awakens longings which this life alone cannot satisfy.

## 21.

# Easter:
# The Community of the Resurrection

> Blessed be the God and father of Our Lord Jesus Christ! By his great mercy he has given us a new birth into a living hope through the resurrection of Jesus Christ from the dead.
>
> *I Peter 1:3*

I want to tell you about a monastic order, the Community of the Resurrection. It has lived out this text in many countries and there celebrated the resurrection. It was founded in 1892. This text often recurs in the liturgy of the Community. In 1898 a small group of Anglican monks moved from Oxfordshire to the mill town of Mirfield between Huddersfield and Leeds in West Yorkshire. Mirfield's buildings were black from the smoke of the factory chimneys and the continuous procession of trains crossing the Pennines between Manchester and Leeds. The industrial setting, the sturdiness of northern life and of northern Anglicanism, together with the Pennine weather, provided a totally different atmosphere from that of a soft cathedral city. This group of brethren called themselves the Community of the Resurrection because they were trying to follow the New Testament church which sprang from the Resurrection. CR (as it is known) believes that it is vital to live a common life that is a challenge to surrounding society, so often individualistic. The brethren witness against greed by living simply and by having no private possessions. Their celibacy is a witness to a society that treats sex as the be-all and end-all of life.

At first, some Yorkshire people mocked the monks. They nicknamed the House of the Resurrection 'The House of Recreation' or the 'House of Correction' or, simply, 'The Gentlemen's Club'. When the monks walked about the town in their cassocks they nicknamed them 'The Petticoat Men'. Today when you arrive at Mirfield station, you walk up past the mills (now turned into flats), the canal (now popular for holidays) and houses still black with a century or more of soot. You get the bus. You ask for the Community of the Resurrection. When the bus stop gets near, the driver shouts out, 'T'Resurrection next stop'. As you get off he shouts again, 'Any more for T'Resurrection?' The sensitive visitor is bound to hear these words as a message from God. Am I trying to live the Resurrection life? What does that mean? Is the church meant to be the Community of the Resurrection?

The Mirfield Fathers are not only concerned with maintaining daily prayer and community life. They are keen to offer the risen life to others. They not only celebrate the Resurrection of Jesus but offer the possibility of resurrection to individuals and communities. One monk, a Zimbabwean, flies to Zimbabwe tomorrow to bring hope and support to the Anglican church there, as it is being severely persecuted by the government. Many congregations have been turned out of their church buildings and have to worship in the open air. CR did impressive work in Zimbabwe from 1914 to 1983, pioneering secondary education for Africans at a wonderful mission station at Penhalonga, but also trekked round forty-two outstations with their churches and schools. In 1903 a pioneer party of three monks set out from Mirfield for South Africa. There, in and around Johannesburg, they built schools, clinics and churches. For seventy years they trained Africans for the priesthood. Their work in the townships was celebrated in the novel and film *Cry the Beloved Country* and by *Naught for Your Comfort*, written in 1956 by their most famous brother, Father Trevor Huddleston. He devoted his life to an international campaign against apartheid. Among his closest friends was Nelson Mandela.

One day in the early 1940s, Trevor Huddleston was walking along in his cassock in Johannesburg. Seeing a black woman whom he knew with her small son, he raised his hat. The little boy was astonished. He asked himself 'What sort of white man would raise his hat to my mother, a black woman?' The little boy was Desmond Tutu.

Desmond nearly died as a child from polio. In the black townships there was much disease because of the open sewage. He first began to be aware of discrimination when he saw black children scavenging in the litter bins for food thrown away by white children. His father was a poorly paid schoolmaster; his mother cleaned and washed clothes for white households. One day the money for his schooling ran out. They turned to CR. From the age of fourteen, Desmond boarded at their secondary school. However, he contracted TB and for twenty-two months he was in hospital, partly paid for by the Community. Fr Huddleston visited him very regularly, and it was to him that he made his first proper confession. This taught him about the crucial role for the Christian of repentance and forgiveness. This was later to be central to his Truth and Reconciliation Commission. CR also trained Tutu for the priesthood. Last Sunday on Radio 4 he spoke of how, as a student, he was assigned to clean the church. As he cleaned, he would come across monks at prayer. Their devotion to prayer made a deep impression. He was also astounded in racially segregated South Africa, where blacks did all the domestic work, to see white monks cleaning floors and washing dishes. CR gave Tutu a vision of the kingdom of God in which there were no divisions of class or race. CR helped him to go to London University. In London he enjoyed stopping policemen simply to hear them say 'sir' to a black man, for he was used to seeing police abusing or assaulting black people.

In 1985, the Archbishop of Canterbury arranged for Timothy Bavin to move from being Bishop of Johannesburg to come here to be Bishop of Portsmouth so that Desmond Tutu could become the first black Bishop of Johannesburg. Later, he became the first black Archbishop of Capetown. Meanwhile, CR joined those agitating against apartheid. Tutu thus believed that justice was at the heart of the Gospel. Once when he was Dean of Johannesburg Cathedral, a white woman swept into the cathedral and, seeing him, exclaimed 'What is that boy doing here?' Police placed him under surveillance, confiscated his passport and discussed assassinating him. He presided over countless funerals of those killed in riots or by police. At one of these he preached to a hundred and twenty thousand people. Again and again his eloquence persuaded crowds not to resort to violence. But for him, as for CR, prayer was central.

As Archbishop of Capetown, he combined a high profile national and international ministry with six hours of daily liturgy and prayer. Having been a regular penitent and much sought-after confessor, he was the ideal choice to preside over the enormously demanding work of the Truth and Reconciliation Commission. This unearthed the evils done during apartheid. The Commission brought together publicly oppressors and victims. Throughout that painful process, he demonstrated his faith that people could change (that is, repent); that people could be forgiven, that ultimately hatred and evil would not triumph. The CR helped to bring resurrection to South Africa both through their own work and through educating and training others, among them Archbishop Desmond Tutu.

His story brings alive today's Gospel. It was the evening of the day of the Resurrection. The disciples had locked themselves in to keep out any who would take them to death, as happened to Jesus. But the risen Jesus appeared: 'Peace be with you,' he said. 'As the Father has sent me so I send you.' He sent them out on a ministry of forgiveness and reconciliation (John 20:19-31). This Gospel passage shows how forgiveness can break in upon people who are trapped by fear and bring them new hope. First of all, they too needed forgiveness for their cowardice, for their desertion of Jesus. Then, like Thomas, people want tangible evidence for resurrection, so we the church must provide it in resurrected lives and communities. Then we can say joyfully with the Epistle: 'Blessed be the God and Father of our Lord Jesus Christ. By his great mercy he has given us a new birth into a living hope through the resurrection of Jesus Christ from the dead.'

# 22.

# Easter: Ascension Day

A text from today's Gospel: part of the prayer of Jesus: 'Father I am coming to you.' (John 17:11)

When President Obama was inaugurated it was an amazing moment for the whole American people, but it was a particularly astonishing event for black people. Forty years before, another black leader, Martin Luther King, had been assassinated. Fifty years ago, many black people were unable to vote. In the south of the United States, black people were segregated from whites on buses and in other public places. Now suddenly here was their man, their man on high, a black man from a race which had been rejected and despised as inferior. There he was among the top people, being inaugurated as President. It had been a bit like that when Nelson Mandela was inaugurated as President of South Africa. The one who had been discriminated against and imprisoned was now on high, president of the whole nation of South Africa, black and white.

We are celebrating the Ascension of Jesus. In the English Missal there is an oddly literalistic picture of the disciples looking up into a cloud with just the feet of Jesus showing. This kind of literalism is unusual in religious art. Archbishop Ramsey used to say that before you can appreciate religion, you must learn to appreciate poetry. On the other side of the coin, the BBC is presenting a valuable series of programmes on the theme 'Why Poetry Matters'. It does matter. Why? Because the language of religion is poetic and metaphorical; symbolic, not literalistic. When we read that a politician is to move into the Upper House, we do not think he will live in a skyscraper. The House of Lords is in fact just along the corridor and on the same level as the House of Commons. Going up is just a way of referring to being ennobled.

The inauguration ceremony for President Obama was a sign that a majority of the American people had said 'Yes' to his elevation. One meaning of the Ascension is that it is God saying 'Yes' to the whole life, ministry, death and resurrection of Jesus, as though God were saying to us: 'Jesus might have seemed just an insignificant Jewish carpenter, but he is my word made flesh; he is king over all things.' In the prayer of Jesus before his death, we hear him twice say: 'Father, I am coming to you.' He takes up to God the whole experience of being human: birth, childhood, adolescence, picnics with friends, hard work running a small business, ministry, rejection, crucifixion, resurrection. How did the disciples know that it was Jesus after the resurrection, that there was continuity between his life before and the life after death? Because his risen body still bore the wounds inflicted by the crucifixion. The Ascensiontide hymn by Bishop Christopher Wordsworth puts it like this:

> Thou hast raised our human nature.
> In the clouds to God's right hand;
> There we sit in heavenly places,
> There with thee in glory stand;
> Jesus reigns, adored by angels;
> Man with God is on the throne;
> Mighty Lord, in thine ascension
> We by faith behold our own.

*NEH 132*

What bold assertions! God has raised our human nature to God's right hand. 'Man with God is on the throne.' That human nature could convey all that we need to know about the reality of God is a great tribute to the capacity of human nature. That is why discrimination against human beings because of their race, gender or sexual identity is so terrible; why corruption, torture, gross inequality all are so offensive. In the mid-1930s Vaughan Williams composed a piece of music to protest against the horrible possibility of war. He called that music 'Dona Nobis Pacem'; that is, 'Give Us Peace'. He chose for the text some verse by Walt Whitman about the American Civil War: 'Reconciliation' from *Leaves of Grass*. A soldier from one side looked at a dead enemy soldier in his coffin and sings: 'For my enemy is dead, a man divine as myself is dead.' Or, as Psalm 8 says: 'You have made us little lower than the angels and crown us with glory and honour.' The Ascension is God's 'yes' to all that Jesus had done and God's 'yes' to the dignity and potentiality of human nature.

I remember vividly when I celebrated the Eucharist for the first time in Africa – in a great basilican monastic church overlooking the Bvumba Mountains of Zimbabwe, near the Mozambique border. I was forcibly reminded that Jesus was just as available there as he is in Portsmouth. The resurrection and ascension freed Jesus to be equally available anywhere. He was no longer confined to the first century streets of Jerusalem or the hills of Galilee. He can be with us here this morning through word and sacrament. Jesus prayed, 'Father, I am coming to you.' What did he mean? Moving towards his Father was the whole direction of his life. In heaven after the ascension he continues that movement, forever offering his life and death for humankind. As the Epistle to the Hebrews puts it: 'We have a great high priest who has passed through the heavens, Jesus, the Son of God'; 'He always lives to make intercession' (Hebrews 4:14; 7:25). This is directly relevant to the Eucharist. At the beginning of the Eucharistic prayer we hear 'Lift up your hearts' – raise your eyes, let go of things earthly and enter into the heavenly places. Thus we pray in the collect for the Ascension: 'Grant, we pray, almighty God, that as we believe your only-begotten Son our Lord Jesus Christ to have ascended into the heavens, so we in heart and mind may also ascend and with him continually dwell.' In the Eucharist, Christ takes us into that stream of love and sacrifice which he ever offers to the Father. As a Eucharistic hymn puts it: 'Look, Father, look on his anointed face, And only look on us as found in him' (NEH 273).

This is what we call the Eucharistic sacrifice. The bishops at the Lambeth Conference in 1958 expressed the nature of the Eucharistic sacrifice succinctly: 'Christ with us offers us in himself to God.'

There is another fine Anglican hymn that we sing which clearly expresses the Eucharistic sacrifice. We shall be singing it here in Portsmouth Cathedral next week at the Anglican-Roman Catholic Day about the Eucharist. It includes this verse which expresses the priestly ministry of Jesus as ascended Lord:

> Now in remembrance of our great Redeemer,
> Dying on Calvary, rising and ascending,
> Through him we offer what he ever offers,
> Sinners befriending.
>
> *NEH 288*

'Through him we offer what he ever offers.'
'Christ with us offers us in himself to God.'

Finally, we come back to our text from the Gospel, 'Father, I am coming to you', and that passage from Hebrews, 'We have a great High priest who has passed through the heavens, Jesus Christ, the son of God.' The Ascension is God's great 'yes' to the life and work of Jesus; God's 'yes' to the glory and potentiality of human nature. Christ is eternally moving in sacrificial love towards his Father in the heavenly places on our behalf. That is what it means to be Jesus, our great High Priest.

# 23.

# Pentecost

Do you ever look at the trees on the road next to the sea, here in Portsmouth? Do you think that is an odd question? If you look at the trees on that road, you will discover that they are all bent in the same direction. The reason is obvious. They are bent by the prevailing wind. In the Bible the Holy Spirit is the prevailing wind, powerful but unseen. We can never see the Spirit, only the effects of the Spirit, just as we can never see the wind, only its effects.

In the Scriptures we don't just encounter the Spirit at Pentecost but in the creation – in the second verse of whole Bible in fact – 'the earth was a formless void and darkness covered the face of the deep, while the spirit of God swept over the face of the waters'. The word 'spirit', there as elsewhere, can be translated as 'a mighty wind'. It was God's Spirit who inspired writers, leaders and prophets. In Exodus 35:30-35 and Wisdom 7:15-30 we hear that the Spirit inspires craftsmanship and scientific discovery. The same Spirit overshadowed Blessed Mary, enabling her to conceive (Luke 1:35). When the risen Jesus ceased to appear to the early Christians, they experienced a special outpouring of the Spirit, who has enabled believers in all places and times to experience Jesus as contemporary, not least in the Eucharist. In today's lesson from Acts the Spirit is likened to a violent wind or to tongues of fire (Acts 2:1-21).

The word Pentecost signifies the completion of fifty days after Passover. This day used to be known as 'Whitsunday'. This title derives from the custom of baptising and confirming new Christians today – they wore white, hence White or Whit Sunday. It was still current enough in the 1950s for Philip Larkin to write his famous poem 'Whitsun Weddings'. People then still talked about 'going away for Whit'. In the Manchester area, where I lived after the war, churches arranged huge processions in the streets called 'Whit Walks'. All traffic stopped. Where can we see the activity of the Holy Spirit in the world and church today? I give you three capital letters so you will remember them more clearly: P.U.L. We experience the Spirit as we move towards Participation, Unity and Liberation.

## Participation

In today's Epistle (1 Corinthians 12:3-13), St Paul likened the church to a human body whose source of life is the breath, the Spirit. During the last hundred years, in both church and society, there has been a huge change with much more participation of the people. It was not until 1928 that all adult women were able to vote in the United Kingdom. Parochial Church Councils only became compulsory in 1919. Church services used to be largely clerical monologues addressed to people meekly kneeling down. By contrast, new liturgies encourage everyone to participate not only by sharing the words, but also by standing more. This expresses our dignity before God, given to us by baptism.

Education is no longer thought of as a teacher at the front trying to fill a lot of empty vessels; rather, we engage in participative learning. Students find out for themselves and bring their findings to small groups. We need a lot more of this in the church. I think of one congregation which after the Sunday Eucharist splits up into groups to study and discuss the lessons and the sermon. It has improved the listening to lessons and sermons. It also improved the actual sermons. Can you imagine us all staying today to a bring-and-share lunch so we can talk about the Holy Spirit together? Or have you had enough of God after an hour? Clergy need to learn a new type of leadership that gives room for lay people to grow and take initiative. This is particularly true of cathedrals, which have traditionally been top down from the clergy to laity. Someone said 'A good leader produces followers. A great leader produces leaders.'

Today's epistle is all about participation in the spirit-filled body: 'There are varieties of activities but all are activated by one and the same Spirit.' The Spirit leads world and church into more participation so that everyone counts; everyone can make his or her unique contribution.

## Unity

There is only one baptism into the one body by the one Spirit. When I was in Queen Alexandra Hospital a few months ago, I was looked after by people of at least six different racial backgrounds. It reminded me of today's epistle from Acts 2: Parthians, Medes, Elamites and residents of Mesopotamia, a long list which concludes with Cretans and Arabs, could hear the Apostles speaking to them in their own tongues. Here on the hospital staff were people whose parents, years ago, were total strangers far away from each other across thousands of miles of land or ocean. Now we have all been brought into one community. Unity begins with an exchange of gifts. We could ask other parishes: 'Tell us how you gather fifty youngsters into your youth group? How can we learn from you in our cathedral?' 'Buddhists, will you help us to meditate better?' 'Jews, will you open to us why your religion at home is so enriching?' 'Muslims, why does fasting play such an important part in your faith?'

In our Anglican Communion, we need help to hold Catholic, Liberal and Evangelical traditions in a fruitful dialogue. We have made some progress. Our Roman Catholic brothers and sisters have a longer way to go. A number of Roman Catholics, clerical and lay, have been severely disciplined for even raising the issue of the ordination of women. Pope Francis, however, has a new, more informal and approachable, style of papacy. He refuses to stand on ceremony and has forbidden congregations to clap when he walks in. The structures of a top-down style of authority remain, but throughout the world, despite many conflicts, the Holy Spirit is drawing us all into one world, so we have been brought near to people of races and religions we hardly had heard of fifty years ago. Having been brought near, how can we grow into a rich unity, both as human beings and as Christians?

## *Liberation*

In the Gospel we hear how Jesus gave his church power to liberate people from their sins (John 20:23). From all over the world, we hear the cry for liberation. Think what a huge contribution women now make in positions of leadership in church and society, yet women were only able to become full members of the University of Cambridge in 1948. We celebrate the liberation not only of women and black people, who were both once treated as inferior; but also the liberation of gay women and men who once had to live under persecution. If everyone participates, everyone counts. This leads to unity and to liberation. Liberation is the key to the Bible: liberation of the Jews from slavery in Egypt; the liberation brought by Jesus. Jesus said. 'The wind blows where it chooses, and you hear the sound of it, but you do not know where it comes from or where it goes.' (John 3:8.)

In 1954, I heard Michael Ramsey, then Archbishop of York, during a university mission, describe his hope that a future successor would be black. Forty years later, in 2005 John Sentamu, a former Ugandan judge, became Archbishop of York. On this Feast of Pentecost, we pray that the Holy Spirit will lead us to participate, so that we may grow into unity and find true liberation.

# 24.
# Trinity Sunday

A pen appeared, and the god said:
'Write what it is to be man.' . . .

        . . . and I spelled out
the word 'lonely'.

*R.S. Thomas, 'The Word'*

Is that true? Maybe we feel we never can fully convey who we are to another person. But if we do feel lonely, isn't that because we know deeply that it is only through close and honest relationships that we are completed, fulfilled? From early times, people have meditated on this theme and have produced various stories to explain our sense that we need to be completed by relationships. The Greek philosopher Plato retold the old myth that originally human beings were both male and female. But the god Zeus split them in half because they were becoming too powerful. That is why we are always searching for the other human being who is that half we have lost.

Couples say: 'here is my other half' – or, if someone is feeling unusually generous, he says, 'this is my better half'. Genesis, in its second account of creation, provides another poetic, mythical story to explain this sense that we are incomplete without relationships. God says: 'It is not good that the man should be alone; I will make a helper as his partner.' When the man saw the woman whom God had created for him for the first time, he said, 'This is at last bone of my bones and flesh of my flesh.' (Genesis 2:18, 23.) In this story, the woman was made out of one of the man's ribs. This was attempting to explain why we need relationships to complete us. But note also that in the other, very different, account of creation in Genesis, God creates man and woman together and says, 'Let us make humankind in our image.' (Genesis 1:26.) Does this mean that the relationship between male and female somehow reflects God's own being, that God is not solitary, alone, but contains a relationship within himself?

On Trinity Sunday we celebrate God who is beyond us as Father, tangible as Jesus, between and within us as the Holy Spirit. In today's Old Testament lesson, we hear Isaiah reminding us of the beyondness of God – his transcendence: 'Have you not known? Have you not heard? The Lord is the everlasting God, the Creator of the ends of the earth.' (Isaiah 40:28.) We hear the same theme in Psalm 97: 'Clouds and darkness are round about him.' The name 'Jehovah' may mean 'Ah!', an expression of awe and astonishment. The seventeenth century Anglican poet Henry Vaughan wrote:

> There is in God (some say)
> A deep, but dazzling darkness.
>
> *Henry Vaughan, 'The Night'*

Today's Gospel (Matthew 28:16-20) presents Jesus as the bridge between God and humanity. The disciples did something which would have horrified other Jews – they worshipped him. The Jewish tradition was absolutely clear: only God is to be worshipped. In any case, Jesus had been declared a cursed outcast by being crucified. Proverbs and the book of Wisdom already had described the mysterious figure of Wisdom who had aided God in creation. St Paul takes this term and uses it to describe Jesus; Christ is 'the power of God and the wisdom of God' (I Corinthians 1:24). John uses a similar term: 'Word' or 'Reason' (*Logos* in Greek). John begins his Gospel with 'In the beginning was the Word, and the Word was with God, and the Word was God.' He goes on to say that in Jesus 'the Word became flesh and lived among us' (1:14). But the disciples had a third experience of God: the Holy Spirit who enlightened them about who Jesus really was, who empowered them to go out to continue the work of Jesus, and who was the source of the fellowship they experienced in the church. The second reading, II Corinthians 13:11-13, reminds us of the words of the Grace: 'The grace of our Lord Jesus Christ, the love of God, and the communion of the Holy Spirit be with all of you.'

We speak of three persons in one God. But what does 'person' mean here? The same Greek actor appeared with different masks, perhaps that of a young man for the first scene, a middle aged man for the second scene, an old man in the third scene. 'Mask' in Greek is 'persona'. That is what 'three persons' means, not three separate individual gods. Rublev's famous Russian icon of the Trinity depicts three distinct beings. But look carefully and you see each one has exactly the same features, and all incline their heads to one another. There are many other analogies. I remember going into a Leeds pub once where there was a marvellous jazz trio, sax, trumpet and double bass all playing together, but from time to time the trumpeter, or the double bass, or the saxophonist would take central stage. Yet the activity of one was the activity of them all: diversity but with a fundamental unity of purpose and spirit.

We need to be Trinitarian in our doctrine, the life of church and our own prayer. Recently I went to the centenary reunion of the theological college at Mirfield. An elderly priest (that is, one even older than I am) had retired near a cathedral. 'I've been going every Sunday for three years, When the Dean sees me, he always bows, but he never says anything or asks who I am. Yet the worship is splendid.' But the worship of a cathedral or church cannot be splendid if we are not seeking Christ in one another; if we know nothing of the fellowship that the Spirit creates. Cathedrals are often good at transcendence, but need to work hard at incarnation, at finding the word made flesh in people, and they need to work hard to find the freedom of the Spirit.

Visiting Zimbabwe, I heard of a famous missionary priest, Arthur Shearly Cripps. He built his first church there in 1911. He was determined that it would not be like a fortress with solid walls. No, he built a roof on poles, so that there was no clear boundary between church and world, and people could come and worship inside or outside or on the edge. Birds could fly in and out. Think of the ways in which the Spirit (often depicted as a dove) has blown new questions towards us. What does it mean for men and women to be equal? How do we understand sexuality afresh? Why do some churches now offer prayers of blessing for same-sex couples who have entered a new partnership? Have we not been blown into realising that social justice and peace making are part of the Gospel? So we need to have a balanced Trinitarian belief.

Glory to the Father, the mystery, beyondness of God. Glory to Jesus, the human face of God. Glory to the Holy Spirit who makes us free and is the Lord and Giver of Life. Glory to the Spirit who takes us to the Father through the Son. Glory to the Father through this Eucharist as the Spirit takes us to join in the offering of Jesus. Glory be to God in his diversity and unity.

# 25.
# Corpus Christi: Five Titles for the Eucharist

Clergy are often thought of as being authoritative teachers. But it is laypeople who are constantly meeting people who are muddled about the Christian faith. You can be teachers as well as clergy can. Indeed, people outside the church will sometimes take more notice of lay people than clergy, because some say that clergy only say this or that because they are paid to do so. It is good, therefore, to have some sermons on basic themes.

Today I want to help you to become a teacher about the Eucharist. Of all the sacraments it is the Eucharist that has the greatest number of different names. I want to hang what I say on these five familiar names.

## 1. The Lord's Supper

The Eucharist was inaugurated in a historical setting. The Last Supper was held just before Jesus went to betrayal, torture and death. The Lord's Supper was instituted during the Jewish Passover. The Passover commemorated the exodus, the deliverance from Egypt. At the heart of the Passover was a meal upon the lamb which had been sacrificed. Jesus, the lamb of God, was offering himself as the lambs were being offered. He wanted his disciples to be drawn with him into the sacrifice offered to his Father in love and obedience.

It would have been natural for anyone facing pain and sacrifice to go inwards and be obsessed with himself. Not Jesus. He goes outward to his Father and to his disciples: 'This is my body which is given for you. This is my blood which is shed for you.'

## 2. Holy Communion, Holy Fellowship, Holy Community

As we are drawn together into relationship with Jesus so we find ourselves being drawn to one another; so we greet each other at the peace; we wait side by side with other people to be fed; then we share the common bread and drink of the common cup.

We are not drawn together by a theory, but by the transformation of material things. Christianity is not a spiritual religion but a sacramental religion: it is about the way God uses material things. Jesus is the Word but comes to us as a man of flesh and blood. In the sacraments, God uses material things: water in baptism; bread and wine in the Eucharist; oil in healing; and hands in confirmation and ordination. I was tidying a room once when I came across several things which my children had made for me when they were young: a wooden aeroplane, a design with my initials in cotton, a sword; it was very moving to hold them again. They'd worked so hard on them sixty years ago. As I held them, my children conveyed their love through those objects to me now. In a mysterious way we cannot explain, Jesus gives himself through bread and wine. We don't receive grapes and corn, but wine and bread: things upon which people have worked, and been paid for.

Every Eucharist provides a vision of a new society in which people discover a new relationship to God through sharing material things, with other people. Holy Communion, holy community.

## 3. Eucharist

'Eucharist' means gratitude, thanksgiving. Just when Jesus might have concentrated upon himself and the awful things which were about to happen, he took the bread and wine and gave thanks. The main prayer of the Eucharist is called the Eucharistic prayer in which we give thanks for all God has done from creation through to the present. However, gratitude is not just the key to the Eucharist. It is the key to life, which means learning to leave our worried selves behind and to look outwards with gratitude.

Giving thanks over the bread and wine consecrates them so they become the means by which Jesus comes to us. Giving thanks daily for our lives and the things that happen to us – even the painful things – enables God to consecrate our lives and our pilgrimage. When we give thanks, Jesus draws near.

## 4. Liturgy

Liturgy is the Eastern Orthodox term for the Eucharist. 'Liturgy' is what we call our morning cathedral worship, which includes the Eucharist. What does the word mean? It means public work. Worship is work done and offered by us on behalf of the community. This reminds us that we're not here to float on a blissful cloud, but here to make an effort: to make the words and actions mean something to us; to remember that we are here for the sake of others. We must concentrate our attention before the service begins, to ponder the lessons. The liturgy is not just for the clergy but the action of the whole community, all of us. The word 'duty' is not fashionable, but it is a word which reminds us that life is not simply about feelings but about obligations: we have duties toward our world, our country, our city.

We pray in one Eucharistic prayer: 'It is our duty and our joy, at all times and in all places to give you thanks and praise.' Come prepared to do some work on behalf of others as well as for yourself: it is our liturgy, our duty and our joy.

## 5. *Mass*

The final title, Mass, is a term used by Roman Catholics, some Lutherans, some Anglicans. In the first Anglican Book of Common Prayer of 1549 this service is titled: 'The Supper of the Lord and the Holy Communion, commonly called the Mass.' The reformers obviously wanted to include a wide spectrum of people, and to make it clear that the Church of England was in continuity with the past. They included, therefore, the traditional title 'Mass'. 'Mass' comes from the Latin phrase with which the old service ended: 'Go, you are dismissed.'

I remember a priest was once asked what the most important part of the Eucharist was: the Gospel? The sermon? Communion? 'No,' he said, 'the most important moment of the Eucharist is when we go out of the door, taking Christ out into the world.' If we use the names 'Lord's Supper' or 'Holy Communion', this puts in touch with the more evangelical Christians; if we use the name 'Liturgy', we are united with the Orthodox; if we use the name 'Mass', we are united with Roman Catholics and some Anglicans. We could prepare for the Eucharist by turning its various titles into prayer. 'Lord, the sacrificed lamb, we will be with you in the Upper Room when we celebrate the Lord's Supper. We look forward to Holy Communion with you and with the holy community on earth and in heaven. We offer this Eucharist to show our gratitude. Through the liturgy we offer our worship and work on behalf of others. Send us out enriched by your word and nourished by your sacrament.'

# 26.
# The Transfiguration (6 August)

The Transfiguration has been a major Feast in the Church of England since the 1928 Prayer Book. But the story remains one of the least-known episodes in the life of Jesus. Is it because the Feast falls in the holiday month of August? It has always meant more to Eastern Orthodox Christians, who celebrate it as the transfiguration of the physical world as well as humanity; an anticipation of the resurrection. For Christians today it is also the anniversary of the terrible light created by the dropping of the first atomic bomb on Hiroshima. We pray always on this day for a transfiguration of relations between nations.

The story of the Transfiguration of Jesus is recorded in all of the first three Gospels. The version set for the Eucharist is Luke 9:28-36. Jesus took Peter, James and John up the mountain with him to pray. It was a crucial stage in his ministry. We can understand it as a retreat before the final conflict. At the top of the mountain, Jesus began to pray. He was keenly aware of the conflict, suffering, and death that was bound to come if he went on with his type of ministry. 'And while he was praying, the appearance of his face changed, and his clothes became dazzling white.' Moses, representing the law, and Elijah, representing the prophets, appeared to support him. They spoke of his coming 'departure' – the Greek word used here is 'exodus', which implies that Jesus is the new Moses, who led the Jews out of Egypt in the exodus. A voice from heaven announced: 'This is my Son, my Chosen, listen to him!' After a moment it was all over. The light and the glory, Moses and Elijah all disappeared. The voice from heaven was heard no more. Then Jesus and the disciples went down the mountain, back to ordinary reality and people in need.

It is impossible to reconstruct what we would have experienced, hearing the story for the very first time. The whole story was told to believers who were familiar with Old Testament images and stories. We should recall the story in Exodus of how when Moses came down from Mount Sinai, where he had been speaking with God, his face shone (34:30). He was transfigured. Peter, James and John saw Jesus in a new light, both physically and theologically. His hidden glory broke out, like the flame from a smouldering fire suddenly shoots forth and then dies down. 'Transfigure' is not a word we use very often. It is used for special occasions, such as: 'When she came to see me she seemed transfigured, I couldn't understand why and then she told me she had just got engaged.' I have met monks, nuns and others devoted to gazing on God who reflect his glory by seeming transfigured. Transfiguration also points us towards key human experiences. Christianity is not an escape into another world, but a new way of seeing the ordinary world, a way of discovering its other dimensions. Artists, film makers, and poets can open our eyes to see a transfigured world; see the world (as we say) 'in another light'. The poet William Blake wrote: 'If the doors of perception were cleansed, everything would appear to man as it is, infinite.' Perhaps one function of prayer is the cleansing of the doors of perception: opening our eyes to hidden glories. Cleansing the doors of perception is another of the wonderful gifts of artists, scientists, musicians, and poets.

Hear a poem by Edward Thomas. Killed in the First World War in 1917, he lived in Steep, north of Portsmouth. There are some fine windows to him in Steep church. 'Adlestrop' shows how an ordinary scene – stopping at a railway station – can be transfigured if we pay attention with cleansed perception, cleansed thoughts, cleansed eyes.

> Yes. I remember Adlestrop –
> The name, because one afternoon
> Of heat the express-train drew up there
> Unwontedly. It was late June.
>
> The steam hissed. Someone cleared his throat.
> No-one left and no one came
> On the bare platform. What I saw
> Was Adlestrop – only the name
> . . .
> And for that minute a blackbird sang
> Close by, and round him, mistier,
> Farther and farther, all the birds
> Of Oxfordshire and Gloucestershire.

T.S. Eliot wrote in 'Little Gidding':

> . . . history is a pattern
> Of timeless moments.

We cannot order such timeless moments. There is a focus so intense that time seems to stop. At such moments, all we can do is to attend, cleansed of all desire to possess what we experience, grateful for a gift of such grace. There are more moments of glory around than we realise. The scientist can astonish us into wonder, for example, by telling us that every atom of carbon in our bodies was once part of a star.

It is perhaps easier to find glory in landscapes than in people, so we must heed Wordsworth who urged us 'to bring with you a heart that watches and receives' ('Tables Turned'). Wordsworth found glory in those on the margins of society. Perhaps he had learned this from the Christian tradition. Certainly Jesus had the capacity and desire to transfigure all he met, and not least the poor and rejected. John Betjeman's depressions, his fear of ageing and terror of death, sometimes lifted enough to allow him, thanks to his deep faith, to experience the transfiguration of unlikely people, as with 'In a Bath Teashop':

'Let us not speak, for the love we bear one another –
Let us hold hands and look.'
She, such a very ordinary little woman;
He, such a thumping crook;
But both, for a moment, little lower than the angels
In the teashop's ingle-nook.

Always, therefore, begin where Jesus began, asking: 'Where is the image of God in this person, a trace of likeness to God, a trace of glory?'

Is transfiguration the key to the Eucharist? The consecration is not the abolition of bread and wine, but God seeing them in a new light, a new dimension, transfigured in the context of the God-given drama of taking, blessing, breaking and giving. God, people and things in the Eucharist are transfigured into a new relationship with each other. The transfiguration of Jesus was anticipation of the glory; not only of the resurrection, but of the consummation of all things at the End. Our glimpses of glory are like the overture in a darkened theatre, as we wait for the curtain to rise and for the real action to begin. St Paul believed: 'At present we see only puzzling reflections in a mirror, but one day we shall see face to face.' (I Corinthians 13:12.) John Keble, the Victorian Tractarian, wrote:

Two worlds are ours: 'tis only sin
Forbids us to descry
The mystic heaven and earth within,
Plain as the sea and sky.

*EH 497*

'Two worlds are ours.' One of Dennis Potter's most successful television dramas was *Pennies from Heaven*, the title taken from a romantic popular song from the 1930s. Such songs were always promising a better, happier life. God does not give us £10 or £20 notes from heaven, but pennies and tokens: glimpses of glory; glimpses of the great Transfiguration of all people and all things.

# 27.
# Our Lady in Harvest (15 August)

I know that it's no longer fashionable to quote Tony Blair. But you may remember that soon after he came to power in 1997, he said his aim was to see Britain at the heart of Europe. His statement shocked some. But English people before the Reformation would have taken it for granted that Britain should be at the heart of Europe. In Portsmouth Cathedral, the first statue on the left in St Thomas' Chapel is of St Augustine, who became the first Archbishop of Canterbury in 597. Where did he come from? Not from Surrey or even Hampshire but from Rome, where he had been prior of a monastery. He wasn't even consecrated a bishop here in England, but in France. Next to Augustine is our patron, Thomas Becket: he was educated in London, Paris, Bologna and Auxerre – and where did he flee to when the king was after him? To France, no doubt on the medieval Brittany Ferries.

Think of other outstanding Archbishops of Canterbury: Theodore, for example, who in the seventh century helped to establish the parish system – he was a Greek. Or Anselm, the great theologian Archbishop in the twelfth century – he was born in Italy and came to us from Bec Abbey in Normandy. Since the Reformation, however, Archbishops of Canterbury have been British. Rowan Williams was unusual in being Welsh.

Of course, we now have John Sentamu as Archbishop of York, who was born in Uganda. This reminds us that we belong to an international, not a national, church. I often attend an annual lecture at Lambeth Palace. This year it was given by Dr David Starkey, a well-known combative historian both in academic circles and on the BBC. The Archbishop, introducing him from the chair, told us that David Starkey's entry in *Who's Who* includes among his recreations, 'treading on toes'. David Starkey, looking at Rowan Williams, made a retort about sixteenth-century Welshmen who came to London to seek their fortunes.

The Reformation cut us off from Catholic Europe – Italy, France and Spain especially. During the Elizabethan period the English developed a new nationalism, a new separate identity, expressed by Shakespeare in his history plays. You will know the passage from *Richard II* about England:

> This other Eden, demi-paradise. . . .
> This happy breed of men, this little world
> This precious stone set in a silver sea . . .
> This blessed plot, this earth, this realm, this England.
>
> *II.i.*

A French visitor to the cathedral asked me, as continental visitors often do: 'Is this a Catholic or a Protestant church?' Looking around, he could not immediately fit the cathedral into either of the only two categories he knew. I always answer that the Church of England describes herself in the 'Revised Catechism' as 'catholic and reformed'. On the one hand, we cherish the essentials of the Catholic faith and practice including the creeds, the threefold ministry of bishops, priests and deacons and the seven sacramental ministries. But we also learned from the Reformation and we are always open to change and new development, as with the ordination of women as priests. If that French visitor had come to an English parish church in the eighteenth century, he would have found it drably Protestant, the pulpit central, not the altar, and Communion only celebrated once a quarter.

What changed? The Oxford Movement in the nineteenth century revived the catholic tradition in the Church of England which had been neglected – so the altar became once more the focus of our churches; candles, vestments, incense, stained glass, statues, the daily offices of Morning and Evening Prayer were reintroduced. Once again we had monks and nuns: all the features we are used to and take for granted. We forget how recently all these catholic features were recovered.

In the 1960s the Second Vatican Council changed the Roman Catholic Church too – Mass was to be in the vernacular; no longer were laity to be passive but instead active participants in both the liturgy and life of the church; theology was to be more scriptural. Anglican liturgy began to change in 1960s as well. There was a remarkable convergence. When we go to a Roman Catholic Mass, even if it is in a language you don't understand, such as Catalan, we can follow it easily. When Roman Catholics visit this cathedral, they say afterwards, 'It is so similar to Mass in our church.' You could say that, in many ways, Anglicans have re-joined Europe. This growing together of Anglican and European Roman Catholic Christianity is both important for the church and for politics. Of course, there has been a coming together of Anglicans and continental Protestants through the Porvoo and Meissen Agreements too, but that's another sermon. Every division or schism not only divides Christians, it divides the fullness of truth. In a schism the two sides take up fixed positions and shout slogans at one another. It is as though some Christians say to Roman Catholics: 'You make too much of Mary, so we won't pay any attention to her at all.' The growing together of churches is also important politically because so many political divisions follow ecclesiastical divisions. The line down the middle of Europe dividing east and west politically is also the line between eastern and western Christianity.

In 1966, the Anglican and Roman Catholic churches embarked on an adventure through the Anglican Roman Catholic International Commission (ARCIC), which consisted of Anglican and Roman Catholic theologians from many countries. They used a new method. Its members tried to get behind the language of the old divisions at the Reformation to see whether there could be an agreement starting not with slogans and the old language but with first principles. There have been reports that display a remarkable convergence on the Eucharist, Ministry, Authority and so on as a result. The most recent Anglican-Roman Catholic Report is entitled 'Mary: Hope and Grace in Christ'. The Report says:

> The Scriptures lead us together to praise and bless Mary as the handmaid of the Lord, who was providentially prepared by divine grace to be the mother of our Redeemer. Her unqualified assent to the fulfilment of God's saving plan can be seen as the supreme instance of a believer's 'Amen' in response to the 'Yes' of God. She stands as a model of holiness, obedience and faith for all Christians. . . . We join in praying and praising with Mary whom all generations have called blessed, in observing her festivals and according her honour in the communion of saints, and are agreed that Mary and the saints pray for the whole Church . . . the twentieth century witnessed a particular growth in convergence as many Anglicans were drawn into a more active devotion to Mary, and Roman Catholics discovered afresh the scriptural roots of such devotion. We together agree that in understanding Mary as the fullest human example of the life of grace, we are called to reflect on the lessons of her life recorded in Scripture and to join with her as one indeed not dead, but truly alive in Christ. In doing so we walk together as pilgrims in communion with Mary, Christ's foremost disciple. . . .
> *'Mary: Hope and Grace in Christ', 54, 71*

Anglicans ought to feel a particular closeness to Mary when we say or sing her song every day at Evening Prayer. It is not just about her – we don't say, 'Mary's soul magnifies the Lord, all generations are to call her blest.' Rather, we say or sing it with her: 'My soul magnifies the Lord, all generations are to call me blessed.'

On Tuesday 15 August, the Church of England will join with Roman Catholics and Orthodox all over the world in celebrating Mary. Our new calendar has followed Roman Catholic and Orthodox custom and adopted 15 August as a feast of Mary. It has many names. My favourite is the one used by Thaxted Church in Essex, 'Our Lady in Harvest', celebrating all she achieved in this life and took into glory. St Paul declared: 'Christ in you, the hope of glory.' (Colossians 1:27.) Surely that is true of Mary. Let us pray in the two collects for this feast of Our Lady in Harvest: 'Almighty God, who looked upon the lowliness of the Blessed Virgin Mary and chose her to be the mother of your only Son: grant that we who are redeemed by his blood may share with her in the glory of your eternal kingdom. . . . God most high, whose handmaid bore the Word made flesh: we thank you that in this sacrament of our redemption you visit us with your Holy Spirit and overshadow us by your power; strengthen us to walk with Mary the joyful path of obedience and so bring forth the fruits of holiness.'

Note that phrase, 'the joyful path of obedience', and let it sing in your heart and mind this week. If you forget the rest of my sermon, at least remember that phrase: 'Walk with Mary the joyful path of obedience.'

# 28.
# All Saints (1 November)

Once I was in a group touring the underground catacombs in Rome. The catacombs were underground cemeteries where the early Christians buried their dead and held memorial services for them. Two American girls in the party could not understand why the early Christians celebrated the Eucharist among the dead. I tried to explain that the Eucharist unites heaven and earth, but for these two Americans only the present was real. The past did not exist for them. Do you think this is a common attitude among young people today?

We saw the simple statue of Jesus the God Shepherd. There was also a fresco depicting the Eucharist. Inscriptions spoke of the mutual prayer between the living and the dead: 'Januaria, may you be well refreshed and pray for us.' We stood in one of the larger spaces with its altar, where some of the earliest bishops of Rome were buried. I thought of the Eucharistic prayer in which we remind ourselves that we pray with the whole company of heaven: 'Therefore with angels and archangels, and with all the company of heaven, we proclaim your great and glorious name, for ever praising you and saying. . . .' This is an echo of the first lesson from 2 Esdras (2:42): 'I, Ezra, saw on Mount Zion a great multitude that I could not number, and they were all praising the Lord with songs.' In the opening verse of Hebrews 12, the writer compares the Christian pilgrimage to a race in a great stadium where we are cheered on by those who have gone before us into the heavenly places, after also running the race: 'Since we are surrounded by so great a cloud of witnesses, let us also lay aside every weight and the sin which clings so closely.'

The leading Roman Catholic theologian, Baron von Hügel told his niece how pleased he was that she was beginning her retreat on his favourite feast, All Saints. He defined it as the feast 'not only of all the heroic lovers of God that have ever lived', but of all 'single heroic supernatural acts – even if and where they remained single' (*Letters to a Niece,* 89.)

I think of that huge and marvellous book *The Shape of the Liturgy* (1945), written by the Anglican monk Dom Gregory Dix. Towards the end, he movingly and eloquently described the contribution to human history of obscure and long forgotten saints. 'There is an ill-spelled, ill-carved rustic epitaph of the fourth century from Asia Minor: "Here sleeps the blessed Chione, who has found Jerusalem for she prayed much."' How lovely, he wrote, if all that should survive of us after sixteen centuries was that we had prayed much, and that our neighbours, who had known us all their lives, were sure that we had found Jerusalem (745).

During the Reformation, the Church of England retained a calendar of saints with their collects and lessons. In 2000, the Church of England added many new names to that calendar: the new books includes many fine new collects for saints' days, old and new. Now we can celebrate more pre-Reformation saints, such as St Teresa and St Thomas Becket: Teresa was a sixteenth century Spanish nun whose writings are still acclaimed; Thomas Becket, to whom this cathedral is dedicated, was an Archbishop of Canterbury who was murdered by servants of the king for acting independently. Becket is a constant reminder of the need for the church to avoid being subordinate to the state. In the new calendar we celebrate heroes from both sides of the Reformation: St Thomas More and Bishop Fisher, who rightly refused to accept the king as head of the church. But we have in the same calendar Reformers like Cranmer (who gave us the Book of Common Prayer) and Ridley. This new calendar gives us the opportunity to celebrate John Donne and George Herbert, priests and poets, and John Bunyan, the Puritan author of *Pilgrim's Progress*. We can give thanks for William Wilberforce, the campaigner against slavery, and Josephine Butler, who devoted herself to the care of prostitutes. Coming to the twentieth century, we offer our gratitude for Dietrich Bonhoeffer, the Lutheran pastor executed in 1945 for his opposition to Hitler, and for Janani Luwum, Archbishop of Uganda, who was martyred by President Idi Amin in 1977.

Brian Frost, a Methodist friend of mine, once described the helplessness and despair created by his myalgic encephalomyelitis. 'In London my greatest solace has been to worship in Westminster Abbey, where I found the history and the faith of centuries seemed to carry me along.' The Post-Communion prayer reminds us of our participation in the heavenly places: 'O God, the source of all holiness and giver of all good things: may we who have shared at this table as strangers and pilgrims here on earth, be welcomed with all your saints to the heavenly feast on the day of your kingdom.'

# 29.
# Christ the King (Sunday Before Advent)

The kingship of Christ did not end when he was no longer on the earth. Jesus said to his disciples before he ascended 'I will be with you always, to the end of time', which are the last words in St Matthew's Gospel (28:20). The ascension was not the end but the beginning of a reign that lasted long after Palestine, long after 33 CE. But where is this kingdom for which we pray each time we say the Lord's Prayer? How do we see signs of his rule in this world which seems so often anarchic, chaotic? Do you ever put food in the box for asylum seekers and the poor by the north door of the cathedral? Do you regard this box as completely marginal to the main purpose of the cathedral? What is its main purpose? To convert people? To fill the pews? To extend the kingdom? Do you think of this food box as being on the margins of the cathedral's activities? Or central to them?

Jesus asks questions of every church: 'What is your ministry to the poor? Are the poor at home in your church? What proportion of your church's income do you give away to charities? What is the main task of your clergy – the maintenance of the church or the building of the kingdom?'

Between the Sunday after Trinity and the beginning of Advent next Sunday, we have the Kingdom Season, which climaxes today in the Feast of Christ the King. There was a remarkable Anglican monk called Herbert Kelly who in the 1890s founded a theological college and a monastic order at Kelham near Nottingham. He was asked what the students studied as they prepared for ordination. He replied that they were there to discover God's activity in the world: what God is doing at the battle of the Somme, in Westminster, or at the docks at Tilbury. This reminds me of the bishop who created an unusual form for confirmations. After the service, he would lead the newly confirmed with the congregation out of the church into the street outside. He would tell them to look for God in the world outside and not just in the church: 'Thy kingdom come.'

Chaplains are often primarily ministers of the kingdom – one chaplain fought for the rights of the poorly paid; a sports chaplain raised questions about the firm which sponsored their sportswear; another protested at the accommodation provided for students at his university. Jesus said very little about the church which grew out of that small group he collected around him. But he was constantly speaking about the kingdom. God's kingdom isn't a state with buildings, frontiers, passports and border controls. His kingdom comes each time you drop some food into that box at the north door, each time the poor receive justice, each time the handicapped are treated with compassionate understanding, each time the rich are taxed justly. The kingdom does not consist solely of Christians but of all who feed the hungry and care for the sick and homeless, as the parable in Matthew 25 reminds us. Those who fed the hungry, clothed the naked, visited the sick, and welcomed the stranger were amazed that, in acting so caringly, they were caring for the king.

However, if you work for the kingdom you'll find you're often at odds with the powerful. That is why we have had tonight that strange lesson from I Maccabees (2:15-29). The king of Syria conquered Palestine in about 170 BCE. He tried to suppress the Jewish faith. Many Jews refused to obey and were killed. If we serve Jesus and his kingdom, it may mean disobeying earthly rulers. There are a lot of monuments and plaques to military men in Portsmouth, but where are the saints of Portsmouth remembered, those who served the kingdom? I am going to tell you about two priests who lived out the prayer 'Thy kingdom come'. This sometimes meant standing against the powers that be. 'I will be with you to the end of time,' says Jesus. His presence is often challenging, unexpected, and disturbing, but always strengthening.

As you go out of Portsmouth by car, you will sometimes have to stop at the traffic lights by the entrance to the dockyard on Market Way. A red brick Byzantine church is on your right. St Agatha's mission began in 1882, sponsored by Winchester College. Fr Robert Dolling, an Irishman, became missioner in 1885. He built the church ten years later. An annual Dolling lecture is given at All Saints on a topic relevant to his ministry. The five thousand people in the parish had a choice of fifty-one pubs and as many brothels. During his ten years at St Agatha's, Dolling wore himself out transforming the area. He created a gymnasium to promote physical fitness and dancing. Two hundred children and twenty old people were fed twice a week by the church. He built twelve almshouses. Often a dozen people stayed with him in his vicarage. He served a communal meal for eighteen on weekdays and for forty on Sundays. Alumni of Winchester College and MPs sat down with thieves, fallen clergy and people just out of prison. Each meal was a vision of the kingdom of God.

In 1895 the great church was dedicated and that afternoon he preached to six hundred men. During these ten years he made enemies. He criticised brewers, closed brothels, attacked military authorities for their treatment of servicemen and encouraged the growth of trade unions. The worship was splendidly dramatic and colourful but also included homely touches – hymns were often sung to popular tunes like 'Annie Laurie'. After ten years in Landport he was worn out and died in 1902, aged fifty-one.

If you look towards St Thomas' Chapel at the east end of the cathedral, you will see the hanging pyx that contains the sacrament for the sick and dying. Christ uses the pyx to radiate his presence throughout the building. If you go nearer, you will see that it surmounted by a crown; a proclamation that Christ is King. This hanging pyx was given in memory of my second Portsmouth priest Bill Sargent, who lived out the prayer 'Thy kingdom come'. When I gave the first Dolling Lecture in 1988, Bill was present as the Area Dean of Portsmouth. Bill was born in 1926. His early years seemed conventional. At the end of the war, he served in the Indian Army. After his discharge he became a policeman, first in Middlesborough, then in Malaya, but the call to the priesthood kept nagging at him. Ordained in 1957, he joined other curates in 1960 to pledge a regular gift from his small stipend to aid the church in South Africa in its fight against apartheid. He arrived in Portsmouth in 1970 to become vicar of North End. He soon made an impression. He preached a memorable sermon at an ordination here, which was based upon a phrase from Psalm 22: 'I am a worm and no man.'

Much of his ministry was discreet, hidden but subversive; turning up the ground around him, as it were. At the centre of his ministry was the belief of the Victorian Christian Socialist theologian F.D. Maurice that the church existed to promote the kingdom. The kingdom of God was here but needed to be revealed. Bill was thus a devoted parish priest, a constant visitor to the sick and needy, but also someone who on his day off would dig his allotment and bake bread while he listened to Haydn. He walked about the parish in his cassock, so everyone would know who he was. He became increasingly aware of how bad the housing problems in Portsmouth were. In 1973 Bill and six others donated £1 each to inaugurate what became the Portsmouth Housing Association. Bill became chairman. It became the major source of social housing in the city, with many thousands of properties.

The Association's work of providing housing for rent was vital at a time when local authority housing was being sold off. He also founded the Roberts Centre for those with housing and personal problems and led the opposition to the annual arms fair here. This was an unpopular campaign in a military city. He would remind people that just as God came to us as a man of flesh and blood, so in the sacraments God uses water, bread and wine; oil and hands. He meant that the material world matters to God. Bill Sargent died in 1989 and was buried in Kingston Cemetery. His headstone reads:

A much loved man
Friend to the poor
He worked to build
the Kingdom of Heaven on Earth.

# II.
# Keeping Faith in God

# 30.
# Remembrance Sunday

To most people, Richmond Castle in North Yorkshire is just a picturesque mediaeval ruin. But on two occasions I went to see some whitewashed cells where conscientious objectors were imprisoned during the First World War. On the whitewashed walls COs had written in pencil their thoughts and prayers. Some were texts from the Bible: 'Love one another as I have loved you' from St John's Gospel (13:3). One prisoner had drawn a picture of Christ on the cross and had written below, 'Every cross seems light beneath the shadow Lord of thine.' I also read about a group being sent to France in 1916, sentenced to death when they refused to fight and later commuted to ten years penal servitude. At that time Britain was being swept by a tide of patriotic fervour. It took great courage to stand against it. The Archbishop of Canterbury and other bishops were not pacifists, but they defended the right of conscientious objectors to dissent. The dedication of this cathedral to St Thomas Becket is a vivid reminder that we must always give our loyalty to God priority over our loyalty to the state.

The calling to be a pacifist is, I think, rather like the vocation to be a monk or a nun, who also express their Christian faith in stark, uncompromising terms. The COs at Richmond identified themselves with Jesus the dissenter, who, as Peter put it, 'when he was abused, he did not return abuse; when he suffered, he did not threaten' (1 Peter 2:23). Over the centuries, the church has been tempted to try tame Jesus so that he no longer would be a challenge, but he always remains the Great Outsider, the Divine Outlaw. On the other hand, he accepted the need for the structures of the state.

We have to recognise that Jesus was able to maintain the stark simplicity of his witness because he refused any position of power, either civil or religious. People ask, 'Can you imagine Jesus firing a machine gun or dropping a bomb?' The answer is 'No'. But then we cannot imagine Jesus as a Foreign Secretary, magistrate, managing director, or even a bishop or parish priest. Has Christianity then nothing to say to those who exercise power, occupy positions of authority, or have to threaten or use force? I offer two themes to ponder: realism and hope.

## *Realism*

We need restraints against our capacity to do evil. Stand on the ramparts and look out to sea. You see yachts, ferries and fishing boats go by. From time to time, a dark grey ship sails out of the harbour, a frigate or a destroyer. They are reminders that all is not well with us, that we are damaged human beings. Some years ago the police in Toronto went on strike. Some were surprised when criminals ransacked the shops. People were astounded and profoundly shocked when all sorts of normally respectable citizens also stole from shops and houses.

On the North Yorkshire coast there is a most picturesque fishing village, Robin Hood's Bay. In high summer you can wander among the lovely old picturesque houses and the cottages on the cliffs with gardens ablaze with colour. Walk down onto the beach, however, and you discover that all that beauty can only be sustained because a massive and ugly concrete wall protects the village from being swept away by the fierce waves of the North Sea. In the 1662 Prayer Book service of Holy Communion, before we hear the Gospel of Jesus we have to consider ourselves in the light of the Ten Commandments – law comes before Gospel. People and nations need tough restraints upon the human capacity for evil. Once war begins we have to guard against the crusading mentality, against jingoism, and against hatred.

In July 1982, a service was held in St Paul's Cathedral to mark the end of the Falklands War. It was a war with a special significance for Portsmouth because many of the ships sailed from this harbour. Archbishop Runcie of Canterbury paid tribute to the courage of those who had fought, but reminded us that 'war has always been detestable' and 'a sign of human failure'. Some were angered by this and by his request for prayers for bereaved Argentinians as well as the bereaved British. He was accused of being unpatriotic, yet he had been awarded an MC for bravery as a soldier during the Second World War. 'Love your enemies,' says Jesus. At every stage we must be working for reconciliation and healing.

My wife and I have sat upon the Normandy beaches and thought of those young men coming ashore on D-Day and of the Germans waiting for them. Both the horror and the necessity of it all swept over us. Yet all around were signs of healing, destroyed villages rebuilt. Germany and France, who had fought three wars within seventy years, are now working together within the European community.

## *Hope*

We need restraints upon our capacity to do evil deliberately or through negligence. What then is our hope? It is dangerous to put all our hope into this or that development. I remember a sermon in Leeds that identified Christian hope with the work of a particular ruler in West Africa – but a week later he was overthrown and shown to be corrupt. Christian hope is not that history is like an escalator which is taking us up to utopia. While we must strive for peace, we must bear in mind the human sinfulness that so easily corrupts our hopes.

The European Union was created after two wars, largely by Christian idealists. But their idealism about their creation led them to become lax about admission to the community and about financial rules. They did not reckon that human greed would lead some countries into corruption. Yet that neither the EU nor the UN has worked perfectly is no reason to abandon them. If what drives us on is idealistic hope in human nature, we will be defeated again and again and we will fall into despair. What should drive us on is a belief that God goes on hoping – that he goes on believing that Project Earth is worthwhile. Therefore we must go on working with God's hope for peace and reconciliation, always bearing in mind the human capacity to harm and corrupt.

You may know that the Menin Gate which records fifty-four thousand names of those with no graves, killed in the Ypres area during the First World War. An old major, a survivor of the war, remarked some years ago that when he visited the Menin Gate it felt like Gethsemane and Calvary all over again. Searching for some meaning and hope in all this suffering, he had found it in the struggle which led to the cross and the cross itself. Realism and hope meet in the cross. Realism about human evil; hope with God that, absurd and shocking though it seems, evil has a part to play in the creation of good.

# 31.
# Bishop George Bell of Chichester
# (1883-1958)

This year (2008) is the fiftieth anniversary of the death of George Bell, who was Bishop of Chichester between 1929 and 1958. He is being celebrated by the opening of a house named after him at Chichester Cathedral, by a series of lectures, by an international conference at the University, by a series of films, and by parish study.

Why is he so important? Why was the international George Bell Institute, now based at the University of Chichester, created a decade ago? Its Fellows (of which I am privileged to be one) try to forward Bell's concerns in many different countries as writers, campaigners for social justice, ecumenists and artists. Apart from being a deeply caring diocesan bishop, Bell was what we would call now a multitasker. There are some three hundred and twenty huge volumes of his correspondence at Lambeth Palace Library. I could mention a dozen issues with which he was deeply involved, but I will select just three: Bell was a passionate ecumenist, a champion of the arts and a courageous prophet.

## Passionate Ecumenist

As chaplain to the Archbishop of Canterbury in the First World War, Bell was painfully conscious that the church's witness was fatally weakened. Like the nations, the church was divided by ancient quarrels. From 1919 he worked tirelessly to bring together the worldwide church into one fellowship. His vision was not simply that Christians should be nice to one another while remaining separate, but that all Christians should share their gifts in one body.

In the 1930s he forged close links with anti-Nazi Christians in Germany. During the Second World War, he kept contact with Christians in Germany through broadcasts each Christmas. During his Christmas 1941 broadcast he said, 'I think of some of you in your homes in Marburg,

Hanover and Berlin . . . I rejoice to hear your voice, Bishop Wurm in Stuttgart, and yours, Bishop von Galen in Münster. . . . Your fellow Christians everywhere are by your side.' After the war he stood by the German church as it expressed penitence over its share of responsibility for what had happened.

Everyone for Bell was a neighbour – Gandhi came to stay with him and a goat was tethered outside the Palace to supply milk. In 1955, he led a pioneering delegation of Anglicans to talk with Cardinal Montini in Milan – later Pope Paul VI. His Christian faith leapt over national boundaries, hence his deep friendship with the German Lutheran pastor and theologian Dietrich Bonhoeffer. When I lived in Chichester I used to picture Bonhoeffer arriving at the station and walking up South Street and into Canon Lane to the Palace. He was executed in April 1945 for his part in the July Plot against Hitler. As he was led away to execution, Bonhoeffer's final message was not for his family or his fiancée but for Bell: 'Tell him that for me this is the end but also the beginning. With him I believe in the principle of our Universal Christian Christian brotherhood which rises above all national interests.'

In the chapel of the University of Chichester, a fortnight ago at the Bell Conference, a young German scholar asked 'Coming to this lovely city I ask: what was it that gave Bell such a passionate concern for Germany for over thirty years?' A verse of a hymn by Bell answers that question:

> Let Love's unconquerable might
> God's people everywhere unite.
> In service to the Lord of light.
> Alleluia, alleluia, alleluia!

*NEH 345*

## Champion of the Arts

Bell said in his Christmas broadcast of 1929 that the visible and invisible worlds were united that first Christmas Day. He quoted the 'wise' observation in Ecclesiasticus (38:34) that for craftsmen, 'in the handiwork of their craft is their prayer'. He believed that the exercise of art is a form of worship. In 1928 he had pioneered the revival of plays in Canterbury Cathedral when he was Dean. Later he commissioned T.S. Eliot to write *Murder in the Cathedral*, about Thomas Becket which was first performed there.

Both in Chichester Cathedral and in churches in the diocese he encouraged a revival of drama, mural painting and sculpture, some by the notable refugee artist Hans Feibusch from Germany. Thanks to the imaginative initiatives by Bell and successive deans, today in Chichester Cathedral there is a great variety of modern art: paintings, stained glass, murals, sculpture; all dedicated to God.

## Courageous Prophet

Bell cared passionately for social justice at home as well as abroad. He campaigned for trade union rights for workers for the East Sussex County Council and supported the protests of council tenants in Brighton whose rents were too high. He always travelled third class on the railways. As Dean of Canterbury he had fostered devotion to St Thomas Becket (the patron saint of Portsmouth Cathedral). Becket had stood against the state. To borrow Martin Luther King's image, Bell believed that the church should be a thermostat altering the surrounding temperature, not just a thermometer registering the prevailing temperature.

From 1933 he actively supported resistance to Hitler. In Germany his friends knew that it was dangerous to refer to Chichester and so he was known there as 'Uncle George'. 'We have had a message from Uncle George.' 'Uncle George will help you.' He raised money to enable German refugees to come to this country, particularly those of Jewish origin, but it was hard work. Many British people were as hostile to refugees then as they are now. To settle one particular refugee took him a hundred and twenty-seven letters. At the recent Bell conference there were members of two German Jewish families he had rescued.

At the beginning of the war he declared that the church was not the state's spiritual assistant, its mere auxiliary, and that it must not hesitate to condemn the bombing of civilian populations for which we had denounced Hitler. In 1943 he condemned the systematic obliteration of German cities. As a result he was excluded from his own cathedral by the Dean on Battle of Britain Sunday. When in 1944 he repeated his condemnation at length in the House of Lords, he received a pile of hate mail. Yet he knew first-hand that some British bomber aircrew were agonised in conscience about what they were being asked to do.

He paid a price for his courage. Like the prophet Jeremiah, Bell was regarded as a traitor. Once, when Bell gave the blessing, a woman shouted out 'Go back to Germany!' Recently, when the previous Bishop of Chichester was talking about Bell in Worthing, a woman denounced Bell as a traitor. Anthony Eden described him in the same terms Henry II used for Becket, as a 'pestilent priest'. Churchill and Eden blocked every attempt by the church to elevate him to an archbishopric and rejected all suggestions that he should receive a mark of national recognition from the monarch.

Like the lawyer in St Luke's Gospel (Luke 10:29), Bell asked 'who is my neighbour?' He replied: my neighbour is a Russian Orthodox, a Methodist, a Lutheran, a Roman Catholic, a Hindu like Gandhi. Who is my neighbour? A painter, a sculptor, a poet. Who is my neighbour? The Jewish refugee arriving without home or money; Germans and British being bombed; the underpaid council worker. Bell was the Good Samaritan. Like his straightforward name, he rang true. We thank God for him, a modern saint and hero of the faith.

## 32.
# Does God Intervene When Disasters Strike?

In recent weeks I have been thinking a lot about how people have reacted to recent catastrophes like the floods and foot and mouth disease. There was one maverick bishop who suggested that the floods were a punishment by God for the immoral state of British society; I haven't heard any such reactions to the foot and mouth outbreak. A century or more ago, however, such attitudes were common.

In 1866 there was an outbreak of foot and mouth around Warminster. The vicar was on holiday in Rome (lucky thing!) but he wrote to his parishioners that he was glad to hear that the Days of Humiliation had been so well observed in Warminster. (On Days of Humiliation people fasted and attended solemn services in church to confess their sinfulness.) The vicar added, 'May we all own this chastisement as a loud call to us to mend our lives, and to walk more closely with our God.' Some farmers not only attended these special church services but also put up magic signs in their cattle sheds to ward off disease – belt and braces, as it were. Were they saying, in effect, 'If Christianity can't help us, perhaps the old pagan gods might?'

A hundred years later, in 1966, I was vicar of a country parish. We had an outbreak of foot and mouth disease. The vicar of Warminster a hundred years before had interpreted it as a chastisement from God. I didn't see it that way. I didn't hold especially solemn penitential services. In fact, there were fewer farmers in church – they were too busy taking scientific precautions against the spread of the disease. Simply to tell these two stories about the very different reactions of church and people to the same disease is to become aware of how much church and society have changed. It is as though God, like a good parent, has devolved authority and given us more control over our environment. We've been given the key to the front door, as it were, even if it sometimes gets jammed in the lock.

A hundred years ago, those who thought any catastrophe was a punishment from God could quote many Old Testament stories to support their beliefs. But they forgot the story of Jesus, who was asked about the eighteen people who were killed at Siloam when a tower fell on them. In response, Jesus asked, 'Do you think that they were worse offenders than all the others living in Jerusalem?' (Luke 13:4.) In Peru there has just been an earthquake. The largest single loss of life was of two hundred people who were at Mass when the church collapsed on them. Is there an irony in that? It reminds me of the famous earthquake in Lisbon in 1755. It killed between sixty and one hundred thousand people. It destroyed almost the whole city and every significant church. Many were killed *in* church, because the earthquake struck on All Saints Day – 1 November. Reactions were divided. Some, including John Wesley, said it was a punishment for the sinfulness of the people. Others said it was odd that God should punish people for going to church on All Saints Day. Should we instead, they argued, look for a scientific explanation? For they could not believe in a God who was vengeful and irrational. Now, of course evil actions usually have evil consequences. A drunk driver may kill himself and others. We pollute the earth and it changes the weather. Someone gets into the habit of telling lies and they are corrupted. God does not save us from the consequences of our actions. A child may pick up a knife; God does not turn the metal to rubber to save the child. A world that was like clockwork could not allow for innovation to take place. But a world that was totally unpredictable would be an impossible place to live in. Water must be $H_2O$ every hour of the day and of the week and every day of the year.

Are there pure acts of God when he acts alone? Well, we might say, 'What about the Creation?' But are such acts rare? For example, when Jesus came, God needed Mary to say 'Yes' to the conception. God needed a mother; a womb. The sacraments are not pure acts of God. They are the result of co-operation between human beings and God. God needs us to provide water, bread and wine, oil, and hands. Most of the time we cannot know absolutely for certain that this or that is a single pure act of God. A father doesn't only act when he seizes his son by the scruff of the neck to prevent him being run over. He also acts towards his son by the constant influence of who he is. His son is quite unaware of his father's regular work that enables him to pay the bills and maintain the house. The little boy goes to the garage and decides to saw a piece of wood. But as he puts his hand on the saw handle, his father's hand closes over his and they saw together. The little boy runs into his mother 'Mummy, look! I've sawn a piece of wood.' The fact is they have sawn it together.

For most of the time that's how things are with us: God is continually at work influencing, helping, and assisting us, but all the time respecting our freedom so we are unaware of his activity with and through us.

This all suggests that we need to re-examine our image of God. All too easily we think of him either as a benevolent grandfather who will never allow any harm to come to his people or as a vengeful irrational martinet. If something bad happens, people complain, 'I've never done anything wrong, why should this happen to me?' Or perhaps we think of God as a puppeteer who pulls millions of strings every split second.

Bill Vanstone, a priest and theologian, suggested a more homely but more disturbing image. He said: think of a mother making a wedding cake of several tiers for her daughter. She has never made a wedding cake before, and she is doing it, not just for anybody, but for her daughter whom she gave birth to, whom she brought up and has always loved. As she bakes the wedding cake and decorates it, at each moment she is poised between tragedy and triumph. Perhaps the icing will not set? Perhaps the dog will rush in and knock it over? But she doesn't give up, because her love for her daughter is what the Bible calls steadfast love. Do you regard that as a rather frivolous, even shocking, picture of God? Yet here in this story are the great qualities of God – generous and steadfast love, self-giving, creativity, and risk-taking. God limited his freedom of action when he created the universe with all its billions of constituent elements and people, each with some degree of freedom to act. A couple who decide to have children limit their freedom to act. God limited himself when he expressed himself through the limitations of a first-century Jewish man. You can't love without limiting yourself. Love and limitation go together.

> Let the same mind be in you that was in Christ Jesus, who, though he was in the form of God, did not regard equality with God as something to be exploited, but emptied himself, taking the form of a slave, being born in human likeness. And being found in human form, he humbled himself and became obedient to the point of death – even death on a cross.
>
> *Philippians 2:5-8*

# 33.
# Social Justice

In tonight's first lesson, the Old Testament prophet Jeremiah rebukes the King of Judah. He condemns those who build their houses with forced labour, which is an offence against justice and love of one's neighbour. He asks, 'Are you a king because you have a more luxurious palace than any other king around?' He contrasts him with his father Josiah: 'Did not your father eat and drink and do justice and righteousness? Then it was well with him. He judged the cause of the poor and the needy; then it was well. Is not this to know me? says the Lord.' (22:15-16.)

This is a startling statement: that the one vital way in which we can know God is to care for the poor, the needy and to promote greater equality and social justice. Hosea, another prophet, imagined God saying 'I desire steadfast love and not sacrifice, the knowledge of God rather than burnt-offerings.' (6:6.) Imagine a prophet turning up at the cathedral and telling us, 'It is wonderful that you sing Howells in B minor superbly, but what do you do for the poor of Portsmouth?' According to Jeremiah, caring for those in need is one of the chief ways in which we know God. Old Testament laws make special provision for the poor. In Deuteronomy we read: 'Open your hand to the poor and needy neighbour in your land. . . . Remember that you were a slave in the land of Egypt, and the Lord your God redeemed you; for this reason I lay this command upon you today.' (15:11-15.) Jeremiah hears God's reminder to the people: 'Don't forget that once you had nothing; you were nothing; you were subject to the whims of your slave masters.'

In Israel during the days of the Old Testament, social justice was not left to the goodwill of the individual. It was written into the law. In Deuteronomy we read that if you make a loan to a poor man and take his cloak as a guarantee that he would repay the loan, you must return his cloak at night so he has something to sleep in. When you pay wages to the poor, you must pay them every day, before sunset, for they have no reserves. When you reap your harvest and accidentally leave a sheaf behind, don't go back to collect it. Leave it for the foreigner, the widow and the orphan. When you shake the olive trees, leave what is left to the foreigner, the widow and the orphan (Deuteronomy 24:12-13, 15, 19-20). Throughout these commandments echoes the refrain: remember, you were a slave in Egypt; once you were also poor, once you counted for nothing too.

Nationally, we have the Church Urban Fund, which funds projects in the poorest parts of our cities, including sometimes Portsmouth. Nationally, and in our cathedral and shops, we have the food banks. When did you last put some food into the food bank here for asylum seekers or the very poor? The movement all over the country to establish food banks has been largely inspired by the churches. What a comment on our society that a proportion of our fellow neighbours need food banks! These efforts remind me of Jeremiah's teaching that when we create social justice we know God.

I go into the Co-op to pick up my paper. I look at the headlines of other papers. There are two papers in particular which are always shouting either 'Send them home' or 'Lock them up'. This year we celebrate the abolition of the slave trade. We should remember how much of our prosperity derived from the cheap labour which the Empire used to provide. When former members of our Empire come to work and prosper in Britain today, we are repaying a debt we owe them for all their parents and grandparents gave to us in their home countries. In our schools and universities we depend upon thousands of teachers and lecturers from overseas. The NHS would collapse without immigrant workers; so would hotels and significant parts of our commercial life. Where would we be without firms like Marks and Spencer, which was founded by refugees earlier this century? People were asked by pollsters 'What proportion of the population are asylum seekers and refugees?' What did they reply? '23%.' In fact, the proportion of our population who are asylum seekers is 2%. The headlines that scream 'Send them home' create hatred and racial violence. The Archbishop of York is a refugee from Idi Amin's Uganda, where he was a judge. A couple of years ago, as he came out of Westminster Abbey, someone in the crowd spat at him and shouted 'Go home!' That appalling action was a product of the hatred stirred up by newspapers and the kind of casual gossip against immigrants which can be heard everywhere.

The other popular slogan is 'Lock them up'. We certainly do that. We imprison far more people per capita than anywhere else in Europe apart from Turkey. Most of our prisons are overcrowded. Many prisoners remain locked up for most of the day. Rehabilitation is almost impossible under such conditions, so over half of all prisoners are convicted of a further offence within two years of release.

Yet there are other ways of dealing with offenders. When prisoners face the victims of their crimes, re-offending drops dramatically. Punishment in the community is often more effective – apart from anything else, it helps to keep families together. A prisoner whose family have disappeared when he comes out of prison is much more liable to fall into further crime. Full-time prison is necessary only for a small proportion of prisoners. The former Archbishop of Canterbury, Rowan Williams, once criticised our obsession with jailing people and said the present system fails both offenders and victims by failing to change the behaviour of many of those convicted. Many prisoners, for example, receive no help with drug addiction, an obvious cause of crime. A recent Roman Catholic report recently pointed out that if prison worked we would be closing prisons, not building new ones. The press sells papers by scaring us – and one way of doing this is to give the impression that crime is out of control. People refuse to believe that a wide range of offences have decreased in number over the last few years.

A young priest in the Truro diocese was concerned about poverty and homelessness in Cornwall. One Saturday and Sunday he did not shave. On the Sunday morning he dressed in old clothes and pulled an old woollen hat over his eyes. As people went to church he sat huddled and depressed at the door. No one spoke to him. They were horrified when he came into church and sat at the back. They were even more horrified when he went up to the lectern to preach the sermon. He took out a mirror and began to shave. He took off his old coat. 'You see,' he said to the amazed congregation, 'I am a human person just like you. Look upon people not with your eyes but with your heart.'

You might complain tonight and say: 'I came to church tonight to hear about God and all I only heard about prisoners and immigrants.' But Jeremiah says to us that if we are to know God we must work for social justice. We can do this by being well-informed, by listening to BBC radio rather than reading tabloid newspapers that run scare stories; by being in touch with our MPs who do care what people write to them about; by offering help to organisations that care for prisoners and immigrants. We should care about society because God is the community in society: Father, Son and Holy Spirit; because the church is about sharing in community; because at the heart of the church's worship is the Communion, the Eucharistic community.

Instead, however, we have a very individualistic and competitive model of society. Jean Vanier has founded many homes for the handicapped in Europe. He tells of a mentally handicapped young man from one of his homes. He entered a race for the handicapped. He longed to win a medal.

He was quite near the finishing post when another runner from another home fell down. The young man put all thought of a medal aside. He stopped, picked his fellow runner up and hand in hand they ran towards the finishing post. Co-operation and compassion are more important than winning the race. Respond to the needs of the poor and outcast, say Jeremiah and Deuteronomy, as well as Jesus. If we do that, we will discover God in the needy and vulnerable.

# 34.
# Psalms

In a fortnight's time, we are going to have 'Back to Church Sunday'. Have you heard of that? It is when we're urged to invite someone who doesn't usually come to church to return with us or to experience church for the first time. Today, very few people are familiar with the language of the church. What would they make of the psalms, for example? How would a stranger to the church react to this verse from Psalm 60: 'Moab is my wash-pot'? Or what about Psalm 42, which worries about the noise of the water pipes? How would visitors react when they heard the choir promise to God most tunefully, 'I will offer unto thee fat burnt sacrifices with the incense of rams' (Psalm 66)?

I feel moved tonight to ponder the psalms with you. Of course, some of the problems we have with the psalms arise because we use a sixteenth-century translation – that is, the Prayer Book version. That old translation, though beautiful, is sometimes inaccurate and uses language which is no longer current. On the other hand, if you come to said weekday evening prayer, you will find that the modern Prayer Book translation of the psalms we use makes obscure passages intelligible. But you may argue that a bit of obscurity a good thing. Isn't that one reason why we use incense? It reminds us in the words of another psalm that 'clouds and darkness are around about Him' (Psalm 97). If God is surrounded by clouds and darkness, then we need symbols and poetry to speak about God – and indeed about all the important things in life. We ought to ask this important question: should people who step straight off the street immediately understand everything in church without help? I put this question to you in the congregation tonight. Maybe you come to Evensong on a Friday and the choir sings Psalm 22, 'My God my God why hast thou forsaken me', or Psalm 69, 'I stick fast in the deep mire where no ground is'. You might think, 'I don't feel forsaken by God'; 'I am not stuck in the deep mire.' Perhaps you don't know that on Fridays, the church chooses psalms that bring us nearer to the sufferings of Jesus.

In Psalms the 'I', the person speaking, is the righteous man. We should remember that Jesus and the early Christians believed that many of the psalms take us into the spiritual battles which Jesus fought. When we say them through the mouth of Jesus, they burn with a deep and powerful new meaning.

Of course, some psalms yield a rich meaning almost at once – 'The Lord is my shepherd' (Psalm 23) or Psalm 103, 'Praise the Lord, O my soul and all that is within me praise his holy Name.' But some psalms present problems because they refer to archaic practices like animal sacrifices or to bits of Middle Eastern geography. But there is another, more serious problem: those psalms which invite us to hate and destroy the wicked. In the 1662 Prayer Book we were commanded to say all one hundred and fifty psalms over the course of the month; so many in the morning, so many in the evening. Now we say a selection of psalms, chosen by the church, so it is possible to omit bloodthirsty psalms or those which seem to look down smugly upon the wicked. But sometimes we are reading a psalm and then suddenly it turns to cursing, like Psalm 137: 'By the waters of Babylon we sat down and wept, when we remembered thee, O Sion.' Then at the end of the psalm, suddenly the speaker threatens the children of Babylon: 'Blessed shall he be that taketh thy children and throweth them against the stones.' We certainly cannot say those words through the mouth of Jesus. C.S. Lewis in his book on the psalms treated it as allegory, arguing that these 'children' are our sins, which begin as whimpering children pleading that they are so tiny, but can turn a person into an alcoholic or a rapist. Lewis expressed his interpretation bluntly, 'Knock the little bastards' brains out.' Does that convince you? Or is it special pleading that totally alters the original plain meaning? Is it better to omit the final three verses, which are bracketed in the 1928 and 1980 Prayer Books?

Once standing on the platform at Munich station, I noticed that there was a train going to Dachau. Just an ordinary town you could reach by train. How, then, could it be a place of unimaginable evil? There is a convent of enclosed Roman Catholic nuns on the site of the death camp who try to be a sign of hope. Visitors to the camp where so many were killed are often shattered by the evil. Many creep into the convent chapel to try to make sense of it, and be healed by this other Christian world of forgiveness, peace and love. When the psalms were in Latin, visitors were calmed and comforted by the beauty and tranquillity of the plainsong. But when the liturgy changed and was sung in German, the nuns faced a real crisis. How could they, on the edge of the concentration camp, sing psalms which spoke so vividly and vengefully of exterminating enemies?

Visitors to the camp often came away with desire for revenge. Should the nuns encourage these feelings of revenge by the psalms they sang? Or rather should they follow the one who prayed for his executioners: 'Father, forgive them, for they do not know what they are doing' (Luke 23:34). The nuns debated whether they should go on singing such verses as these from Psalm 18: 'They shall cry, but there shall be none to help them: yea even unto the Lord shall they cry, but he will not hear them. I will beat them as small as the dust before the wind: I will cast them out as the clay in the streets.' But the nuns found no simple solutions, for there are no simple answers.

How far should we adjust our readings from the Old Testament so they fit in with Christian belief? Last Sunday evening, the lectionary omitted a particularly horrible story of cannibalism which took place during a siege of Jerusalem (2 Kings 6:28f). Was it right for the lectionary to omit that? (2 Kings 6:24-5; 7:3-end) The nuns obtained permission to omit verses in the psalms they found objectionable. The Church of England in 1928 and 1980 revised its Prayer Book and it, too, put brackets around certain verses it found objectionable. But the church in the 2000 Prayer Book has abandoned the practice of bracketing.

Two lessons can be learned:

1. Since Jesus is the full revelation of what God is like, we must judge Scripture in the light of the character of Jesus: for there are elements in Scripture that are sub-Christian – and not only in the Old Testament. In Revelation there are marvellous passages but also passages which are sadistic and sub-Christian.

2. We need to pay close attention to what we are saying and singing. We are not really worshipping if we glide along in a dream.

I have said psalms at morning and evening prayer daily now for nearly sixty years. I would not like to give the impression that the psalms are only a source of problems. From the death camps arose a great cry of anguish, 'Where is God?', as God's ancient people were gassed in their millions, men, women and children. This was memorably expressed in *God on Trial*, a BBC programme about a group of Jewish prisoners awaiting execution. Why was God silent and helpless? they asked. In *God on Trial*, as the prisoners waited for the gas to be switched on, you could see them repeating verses from the psalms. Psalms minister to us in every situation, even the worst we can imagine. There are many verses which can be taken into our prayers and repeated slowly like dissolving a lozenge on the tongue. I give a few examples:

Thou shalt show me the path of life; in thy presence is the fullness of joy: and at thy right hand there is pleasure for evermore. (16:12.)

Thou also shalt light my candle: the Lord my God shall make my darkness to be light. (18:28.)

O taste, and see, how gracious the Lord is. (34:8.)

Hold thee still in the Lord, and abide patiently upon him. (37:7.)

We wait for thy loving kindness, O God: in the midst of thy temple. (48:8.)

With honey out of the stony rock should I have satisfied thee. (81:17.)

Why not make your own anthology of verses from the psalms, and then use it regularly in your prayers?

If you do that, you will be conscious of millions of people from every age since they were written, gathered round you and joining with you.

# 35.
# D-Day Commemoration

Those of us at home on 6 June 1944 knew something very important was happening, for we heard John Snagge's authoritative voice on the BBC. John Snagge only appeared for very special occasions. Hearing that voice, we wondered 'Is it D-Day at last?' Those who guessed that their relations and friends were in the invasion force heard the news with dread as well as excitement. Wives and families spent a lot of the war waiting and dreading. How different it was for those actually there! One remembered: 'As we got near, there was a lot of gunfire. . . . Then suddenly it was time to jump down the ramp into the sea. On the beach there was chaos. . . . Enemy fire was sweeping the narrow strip of sand. . . . Everywhere there were broken down and blown up tanks and people.' The brigade's Church of England chaplain already lay wounded on the beach. All but one of that brigade's chaplains were wounded that day. At another beach, the landing craft slowed down a thousand yards off shore. The army commander asked why they were stationary when they were under fire. 'There's still five minutes to go,' the captain replied. The commander shouted back: 'I don't think anyone will mind if we land five minutes early!'

A few years ago I visited one of those beaches. I tried to imagine what it was like to be in a landing craft and to see the ramp being lowered. I stood on one of the seaside streets and tried to imagine what it was like to be a French civilian on D-Day. I stood in one of the German pillboxes and looked out to sea. On the beach I saw a plaque *'nos liberateurs'* – 'To our liberators'. An extraordinary tribute by one nation to another, especially remarkable when we remember how proud and self-sufficient the French are, and recall centuries of Anglo-French conflict. *'nos liberateurs'*. How ironic. When Jesus stood up in the synagogue at Nazareth he chose to read a passage from Isaiah (61:1) which we heard as our first lesson. Jesus saw this passage as a summary of his ministry which was just beginning. He proclaimed himself the great liberator: 'The Lord has sent me to proclaim release to the captives . . . to let the oppressed go free.' (Luke 4:18.) D-Day was the beginning of the liberation of Europe from tyranny and oppression.

I want us to reflect how in all sorts of extraordinary ways, the war created unexpected neighbours. Wartime relationships were often unpredictable. You were just getting to know someone and they disappeared to an unknown destination or were wounded or killed. Wartime songs echoed this unpredictability. 'We'll meet again, don't know where, don't know when.' 'I'll whisper while we're apart / Goodnight wherever you are.' I knew a soldier called William who was part of the advance across Normandy in 1944. He got to know very well someone who fought beside him. One day, his friend was badly wounded. William had to leave him behind to be cared for by others. After the war, he wanted desperately to know what had happened to him. He searched for his friend with increasing anxiety. Finally, he found his friend's name on a memorial. At last he knew where his body lay. He felt that his friend was safe, because he was named on a stone, and so would be always remembered.

This is a service of thanksgiving and remembrance. But we who remember today will also die. If we are no longer here to remember, who will? Ultimately, the question is 'Does God remember?' St Augustine wrote: 'Blessed are those who love you, O God, and their friends in you and their enemies for their sake. They alone will never lose those who are dear to them, for they love them in one who is never lost, in God.' In the second lesson today (Revelation 7:9-17) we were given that vision of heaven with 'a great multitude which no one could count, from every nation, from all tribes and peoples and languages. . . . Who are these? . . . They are they who have come out of the great ordeal . . . he will guide them to springs of the water of life, and God will wipe away every tear from their eyes.' Unexpected neighbours in heaven, unexpected neighbours on earth as well.

A lieutenant in charge of three tanks landed in France three weeks after D-Day. At night he and his crew sheltered under the apple trees of Normandy and were kept awake by apples dropping onto the tanks. They were soon involved in heavy fighting. It was at this time that he finally made up his mind to become a priest. He went on to win the MC for bravery. His name was Robert Runcie. Later he became Archbishop of Canterbury and his fellow soldiers discovered they had had an unexpected neighbour. For some, war destroyed faith. For others, like Robert Runcie, the experiences of war strengthened their faith and made them determined to build a better world.

Unexpected neighbours. A British soldier hated Germans for having killed his mates. He advanced to a German position. All the Germans were dead. But around their bodies were letters from their families and family photographs. He suddenly realised these Germans were also human beings and caught up in the same tragedy as himself. Unexpected neighbours. My father-in-law was captured at Calais in 1940 and spent five years as the senior British officer in a German POW camp. Unlike some POWs, he and his fellow prisoners were well treated. Among his papers after his death was found a photograph of the German commandant. After the war they had corresponded. Unexpectedly, they had found themselves neighbours. Thank God that the nations of Europe, who for centuries were at war with one another, are now bound together as neighbours in a community.

At home, too, the war created unexpected neighbours. People from different backgrounds were brought together in the same shelters by a sudden air-raid. Thousands of children were evacuated from cities like Portsmouth, which were in danger from air raids. When those who were better off accommodated the very poor children from the inner cities, they were horrified to discover the huge gulf between the classes. Prime Minister Neville Chamberlain (who at one time had been Minister of Health) confessed with shame that he had not known the conditions under which his neighbours lived. Wartime songs yearned for a better world after the war: 'There'll be blue birds over the white cliffs of Dover, tomorrow just you wait and see. / There'll be love and laughter and peace ever after, tomorrow when the world is free.' Wartime films also looked forward. In *Dawn Patrol* (1941) one Home Guard says to another that there must be a new society after the war. 'No more chaps hanging around for work that doesn't come – no more slums . . . no more half-starved kids. . . . We found out in this war as how we were all neighbours, and we aren't going to forget it when it's all over.' He ended with a quotation from the Old Testament: 'The old men shall see visions and the young men shall dream dreams.' (Joel 2:28)

'We found out that we were all neighbours. . . .' In 1942, both William Beveridge in his Report and his friend William Temple, the Archbishop of Canterbury, provided detailed and radical proposals for a new society after the war. The welfare state and the NHS resulted from the wartime discovery of how (in the words of the film) 'we were all neighbours'. So were fulfilled God's promises we heard in the lessons from Isaiah 61 and Revelation 7: 'They shall repair the ruined cities, the devastations of many generations. . . . God will guide them to springs of the water of life and God will wipe every tear from their eyes.' Thank God for bringing good out of the evil of war.

# 36.
# World Faiths

In tonight's first lesson, Jeremiah the prophet denounced the worship of physical idols (10:1-16). Jeremiah argues that God can never be represented by physical idols, for he is always greater than our images of him. It is true that any images we have of God, whether physical or mental, are inadequate. Christians would say 'Amen' to that. However, religion is always more complex than one might at first think. In Judaism, though images of God are forbidden, Jews use many physical means by which to serve and worship him – the biblical scrolls, the sacred meals, the repeated bowings during prayers. For Christians, the coming of Jesus in the flesh has given us a physical representation of the Word of God, yet through belief in God the Trinity, the beyondness, the inscrutable aspect of God is also preserved. Hindus highly value physical representations of the gods. I remember a television programme about Hinduism that focussed on an Indian village which annually saw the making of a statue of a divine figure. It was carried through the streets to a shrine. Candles were lit before it, food was offered to it. After a set period, it was removed from its shrine, carried through the streets on a cart, then ceremonially dumped into a pond, and people trampled on it. Was this saying that images are essential, but in the end quite inadequate? Over the centuries, religious people, including some Christians, have taken a dismissive attitude to other faiths. How should we regard other faiths? This is what I want to open up tonight.

In recent years before Christmas, here in the cathedral we have organised a gathering with Muslims from the Wickham mosque to celebrate the birth of Jesus. One year we walked together round the cathedral looking at various objects. When a Muslim and I came to the lectern I stopped and pointed out the Bible. I explained that the Christian Bible also included the Jewish scriptures and that we used parts of the Jewish scriptures at services every day. She was astonished. 'I had no idea,' she said. We are so used to the fact that our Bible contains the

Jewish as well as the Christian scriptures that we have forgotten that it is unique. The Bible is the only holy book in the world which contains the scriptures of two different religions. The earliest Christians were Jews and this meant that they had to interpret their Christian faith in the light of their Jewish faith. Jesus himself was a Jew and found his mission and identity through the Jewish scriptures which he often quoted, but he also claimed the right and authority to correct them. 'You have heard that it was said to men of old "You shall not murder". But I say to you that if you are angry with a brother or sister you will be liable to judgement . . .' (Matthew 5:21-2). Jesus was grateful to be fed by the Jewish scriptures, but was also prepared to correct them. He was prepared even to stand against Moses on issues such as divorce. On the one hand, early Christians wanted to point out that the Christian faith was new; on the other hand they wanted to stress its continuity with the Jewish faith. How could they account for all that was good and holy in the faith that had nurtured them? They believed that God had been continuously at work and revealing himself ever since the creation.

At the beginning of St John's Gospel we don't immediately hear about a nativity. Instead we hear about God's Word, God's message which had been at work from the creation onwards. This divine Word enlightens everyone, says John, not just Christians, not just Jews, but everyone: it was this divine Word, this divine reason who was made flesh in Jesus. Christianity is thus literally almost as old as the hills. It is not just a faith which sprang into being with Jesus. St Paul in 1 Corinthians 10 meditates on the way God led his people through the wilderness and then makes the startling comment, 'they drank from the spiritual rock which followed them, and that rock was Christ' (10:4).

It is astonishing that not only does the Bible contain the faith of two religions but that the Bible contains elements of other religions too. The basic themes in the two creation stories in Genesis 1 and 2 come from Babylonian religion. Many of the psalms were originally sung to Baal the Canaanite God and have been reworked for Jewish use. Much of the book of Proverbs is similar to collections of proverbs in other countries of the Middle East. Abraham's son Isaac had an Egyptian mother and wife. King David was the product of a mixed-race marriage. The Bible, and hence our faith, is fed by other religious streams. Therefore Christians are in an excellent position to respond to a multi-faith society and world because they have a Bible and faith fed from several religious sources.

I once lived near St Albans Cathedral. Looking at the building casually you might imagine it was all built at the same time. In fact, some of the bricks were taken from buildings in the old Roman town, so they are nearly two thousand years old. 'Old stone to new building,' as T.S. Eliot says in the 'Four Quartets'. So it is with the Bible: there are many layers of many different dates from many different sources. At one time I taught world religions for the Open University. I was convinced that Christians are able to hold fast to Christ as God's Word made flesh while gratefully acknowledging the work of God in other faiths.

When a Muslim was appointed as head of religious broadcasting at the BBC, there were some eyebrows raised. But a Sheffield vicar welcomed the appointment. He spoke of how there had been a large comprehensive school in his parish. Its headmaster was Muslim. This Muslim head wrote to the local vicar and said that the school included students of a dozen different religions, all of whom knew what their faith was. The only children who had no religious knowledge or allegiance were the whites. The Muslim head asked the vicar to come in regularly to take Christian assemblies and to teach them about Christianity. This is but one of many examples where Muslims put Christians to shame because they take their faith more seriously. Contrast the rigours of Ramadan with the easygoing way most Christians keep Lent. Mosques are full of men. The majority of worshippers in Christian churches are women. Perhaps God has sent Muslims to this country to teach Christians what faith is and what it costs.

George Appleton was for many years a missionary in Burma, and later Archbishop in Jerusalem. He wrote in *On the Eightfold Path* that when he sailed to Burma in 1930, as he stepped down the gangplank he thought that he was taking Christ with him to the people of Burma. 'Now,' he said, 'I would step down that gangplank with a very different attitude: I would spend the first year trying to discover how Christ was already at work in Burma unseen and anonymously.' Max Warren, another great missionary and head of the Church Missionary Society, was quoted in Peter Schneider's *Sweeter Than Honey* (12) as saying: 'Our first task in approaching another people, another culture, another religion, is to take off our shoes, for the place we are approaching is holy. Else we may find ourselves treading on men's dreams. More serious still, we may forget that God was here before our arrival.'

In the first niche behind St Thomas' altar we have the figure of the first Archbishop of Canterbury, Augustine, who arrived in Kent in 597. Pope Gregory the Great, who sent him, told him not to destroy all the pagan religious sites and customs but to build on them. Sprinkle the temples with holy water, he said, and use them for Christian worship. Today we know how at Christmas we have sprinkled holy water (as it were) on such pagan customs as holly and mistletoe – indeed, Christmas itself was originally a pagan festival which Christians took over. Most religions have much in common, but there are still significant differences between them. The Chief Rabbi Jonathan Sachs pointed out that in the Bible we are commanded to love our neighbour on only one occasion, but we are commanded to love the stranger by thirty-seven different texts. It is not too difficult to love the neighbour when he or she is like us. Loving the stranger is much more difficult when he or she is *not* like us – different religion, different customs, different colour. But we must look for the image of God in that person who is so different. Our society could become an example to the world of how differences can enrich us rather than cause enmity. We should pray that the appointment of the first Muslim head of religious broadcasting at the BBC will be an example of this.

# 37.
# Marriage

A controversial letter from twenty-seven Roman Catholic theologians appeared in the *Times* on 13 August 2012. These theologians said it was 'perfectly proper' for Roman Catholics to support marriages between people of the same sex. For some this was an appalling statement. For others it was a wonderful liberation. Those opposed to same-sex marriages argue that marriage has never changed. They say that the Bible teaches that marriage is a lifelong union between a man and a woman which produces children. When we actually look at the Bible, however, we discover that many people were polygamous. King Solomon had seven hundred wives and three hundred mistresses – obviously a man of considerable stamina and patience. Herod the Great – the king when Jesus was born – was badly off with only ten wives. On the other hand, there is a great biblical tradition that God was like a faithful husband to Israel even though Israel was often unfaithful.

In today's Gospel, Mark 10:2-16, Jesus takes the people back to the second story of creation in Genesis 2:18-24. Moses had provided for divorce, but Jesus says, 'what God has joined together, let no-one separate'. He doesn't say whether Moses's provision for divorce should continue. The early church found Jesus's early teaching about divorce difficult. In Matthew, later on, Jesus was said to allow divorce for 'unchastity' (5:32). St Paul allowed remarriage if an unbelieving spouse separated. The church throughout history has found it difficult to put Jesus's earliest teaching into practice. Divorce wasn't the only problem. In the first chapter of Genesis, containing the first account of creation, man and woman were created together: they were equal. In the second chapter, however, we have a different account of the Creation in which the man is created first and the woman is created through an operation on him under anaesthetic. God took a rib and from it made the woman. Some down the centuries have argued that this shows that women are subordinate. This has been used as an argument against giving women the vote, or giving women equal education, or ordaining women. Amazingly, Cambridge only admitted women to degrees in 1948. Even today, the conservative evangelical diocese of Sydney has rewritten the marriage service so that the bride vows to submit to her husband.

A few yards from here at the Sally Port, on 14 May 1662, a Portuguese princess named Catherine arrived, suffering from seasickness, to marry King Charles II. The marriage had been arranged for them. They had never met. She gave him the rights to Tangier and Bombay, trading advantages in Portugal and a dowry of two million cruzados. This church was in ruins, so they had to marry in the governor's house near what we call the Garrison Church. There is a copy of the marriage certificate near the cathedral bookshop. They had no children. He had mistresses and thirteen illegitimate children. Royal marriages included political and financial transactions; middle-class weddings, too, often included transfers of money and land.

Dramatic changes in the understanding of marriage are revealed in successive prayer books. In 1662, the first purpose of marriage is the procreation of children. What it called 'mutual society, help and comfort' was relegated to only the third purpose of marriage. The bride also promised to serve and obey her husband. But people grew to believe that marriage should chiefly provide loving friendship and companionship. In the 1928 service the bride no longer had to promise to obey her husband. In the marriage services of 1980 and 2000, having children remains part of the purpose of marriage but it is no longer its chief purpose. Rather, it is mentioned in the context of the whole relationship.

Thus people expected more and more from marriage – not just a commercial arrangement, not a clear hierarchy between a commanding husband and an obedient wife, but a loving relationship between equals. This put new strains on marriage and more broke down. How did the churches react? The Eastern Orthodox Church allows their members to marry again up to three times. Roman Catholics have developed a complex system of annulments whereby a couple's marriage can be annulled because of an inability to carry out the vows. The Church of England has gradually developed a new approach. In certain cases the priest thinks that it is most appropriate for some divorced couples to have a civil marriage followed by a service of blessing in church. Remarkably, this was thought to be the most appropriate service for Prince Charles and Camilla. In the past who would have thought that this was the way to treat the heir to the throne? In other cases it is thought right to celebrate second marriages in church. The priest must be satisfied that the couple recognise the gravity of their new marriage, show penitence for the past and evidence that all previous commitments have been resolved – like the care of any children.

The fact that marriage is understood more and more as a loving relationship that may or may not include having children has influenced our new understanding of gay relationships. Some five per cent or so of the population identify themselves as gay. Civil partnerships enable people to promise faithfulness to one other and provide a barrier against promiscuity. If we can marry or remarry people in church because a faithful loving relationship is the essence of marriage, should we marry gay people as well? I know a woman priest who has served in demanding parishes. For twenty years she has been sustained in her ministry and life by a loving relationship with another woman. I know a much older male priest. He is now in an old people's home after nearly fifty years of a faithful relationship with another man who is now dead. This enriched his ministry and life. In their old age the priest regularly pushed his companion out in a wheelchair – a visible sign of a caring relationship. Is it appropriate to think of such relationships as marriages?

The language of marriage is not confined to marriage. The relationship between a person and God has been described as marriage. Some nuns are dressed as brides when they take their vows – they become 'brides of Christ'. There is the traditional marriage vow: 'I, John, take thee, Mary, to be my wedded wife, to have and to hold from this day forward, for better for worse, for richer, for poorer, in sickness and in health, to love and to cherish.' What is important? Faithfulness and unconditional love. We use vows to express our relationship to God at baptism, confirmation and every act of Communion: we take God for better for worse, richer and poorer, in sickness and health. The language we use about marriage applies to much of human life.

# 38.
# Sabbaths

'Observe the Sabbath day and keep it holy,' says the fourth command-
ment (Deuteronomy 5:12). The word 'Sabbath' means to desist, to stop,
to cease normal activities, especially work. But these are negatives. The
idea of the Sabbath is positive: stop in order to attend to God and his
creation.

The origins of the Sabbath are obscure. One version of the Ten
Commandments (Exodus 20:11) cites as its origin the story at the end of
the first creation story in Genesis: 'So God blessed the seventh day and
hallowed it, because on it God rested from all the work that he had done
in creation' (Genesis 2:3). The observance of the Sabbath was, and still is,
one of the most obvious observances of the practising Jew. Its meaning
was expressed beautifully by an American theatre director, Herman
Wouk, in his book *This is My God*. He wrote that the Sabbath observance
cuts across his life most sharply when he is directing a play. Again and
again on Friday afternoons the play in rehearsal seems to be tottering on
the edge of collapse. He has sometimes felt like a traitor when he leaves
the cast to flounder alone. When he returns home, his wife and sons are
waiting. In the stress of work he had almost forgotten their existence, but
there they are waiting for him in their holiday clothes. They all sit down to
a splendid meal. The telephone is silent. 'I can think, read, study, walk, or
do nothing. It is an oasis of quiet. . . . My producer one Saturday night said
to me, "I don't envy you your religion, but I envy you your Sabbath"' (46).

Christians are not commanded to observe Friday night and Saturday
in that way. But we are committed to what the Sabbath stands for:
desisting, resting, like God contemplating and enjoying. Jonathan Sacks,
the former Chief Rabbi, wondered why he defended the hour and a
quarter on Sunday evenings with no television (which once existed)
when it was threatened, why he allied himself with Christians who tried
to stop big stores opening on Sundays. Why should he, a Jew, care for
what people did on Sundays? Because, he answered, a civilised society

needs pauses, breaks, intervals, a day without work, without spending, a day in which customers did not deprive shop workers of their rest. The destruction of Sunday fills him with the same kind of sadness as when he sees a church pulled down to make way for a supermarket to be built. We need physical reminders that there is more to life than shopping and acquiring.

Angela Tilby was a television producer. In 1998 she was ordained as a priest and we now hear her regularly giving her 'Thought for the Day' on Radio 4. In her book *Let There Be Light* she meditates on the book of Genesis. She keeps coming back to themes which we have just been outlining. Life, she says, oscillates between activity and passivity between work and rest. Night comes and we are given permission to be tired and helpless while sleeping. Holidays are not given to us so that we can recover from work in order to go back to work refreshed. They are to be enjoyed for their own sake as play days. Rest and contemplation are as much a characteristic of God as activity. Blessed are those who have time for us because they are not always busy.

'Observe the Sabbath day and keep it holy.' One approach is to ask, 'What do we do to make Sunday a different type of day?' But we need to ponder the Sabbath principle, that we need to oscillate between rest and activity. Our public worship is often breathless and busy. All that we do in worship needs to be surrounded by silent attentiveness. I realised this summer that I am too busy, with many commitments outside the area, working for the Open University and researching and writing the centenary history of the Community of the Resurrection, as well as my work for the diocese as Diocesan Theologian and here in this cathedral as an honorary priest. I decided to carve out two Sabbath periods of three or four days each time in the next few months.

The first was designed to explore painting pictures. I spent three days with a painter in the Isle of Wight. This was my second visit to him. I wanted to do something that was not about reading and writing, which use only one side of my brain and take up most of my time. I knew he'd taught prisoners at Albany Jail, so I thought he might succeed with me. He taught me to spend seventy-five per cent of my time looking at the object and only twenty-five per cent of the time actually trying to paint it. For me, painting grew into a type of prayer, a Sabbath, for I was really looking, gazing at a stone, a tree, the sky, a plant, a bottle, or a piece of pottery. I saw this as entering into the contemplative side of God, looking, paying attention, giving love and gratitude. This kind of contemplative prayer, being silent before God is one way to keep alive the principle of the Sabbath.

The second was the four days I stayed with the Franciscans at their house near Cerne Abbas in Dorset. I was carried by the daily worship offered in the chapel. All sorts of people gather there: tramps, a bishop, a priest or two, lay companions of the community, people lately out of prison. It is a marvellously equal society, a sign of the kingdom of God where all distinctions drop away, as we gathered at the same altar and ate our meals at the same table. I painted and listened to tapes of poetry and walked in the countryside of Thomas Hardy's novels. With the Franciscans, and in the Isle of Wight, the most important and healing feature of my two Sabbaths was silence. It was, first of all, a 'No', a desisting, but it was a 'No' in order that I might listen, hear God more clearly, detect what was going on inside me, hear the sounds of creation, the birds, wind in the trees, tractors ploughing the fields, the cries of sheep and pheasants.

Archbishop Michael Ramsey used to describe a retreat as a rest towards God. That is also a good definition of a Sabbath, a rest towards God, a rest *for* God so God can be heard and worshipped. If we run away from Sabbaths, from pauses, from silence, from resting, is this because we are afraid, even terrified, of emptiness, or are we frightened that we might hear God? Do we keep busy to distract ourselves from thinking about our death, the ultimate Sabbath, the ultimate lying down to rest from which there is no escape? Angela Tilby in her book includes a chapter, 'The Sleeping Lord', in which she says: 'The God of Genesis . . . stands back from what has been made and takes a break. God rests, God enjoys. And God makes it a rule of the busy universe that rest and passivity should be built in as the most essential part of the timetable. The seventh day is sacred time, playtime and the heart of time. It is the key to time because it is about completion. Work then, for God, is not an end in itself.'

# 39.
# Walls

So the wall was finished.

*Nehemiah 6:15*

Archbishop Rowan Williams has said that we 'are compulsive dividers, separators', but that Jesus bridges these divisions (*The Dwelling of the Light*, 30). The Jewish leader, Nehemiah organised the rebuilding of the protective wall around Jerusalem, which was completed in the autumn of 445 BCE. Fifty years or so before, Jerusalem had been captured, ravaged and its people deported by the Babylonian army. To us, walls are tragically familiar, but Jesus leaps over walls and abolishes divisions. Walls are built to keep some people in and to keep other people out. We picture the Berlin Wall and those who died trying to escape. We remember the roar of joy and the shouts of liberation when it was pulled down.

We were in South Africa in 1983, when the walls of apartheid were high and unyielding. My wife discovered that it was impossible for her to travel into Johannesburg on the same bus as a black bishop who was staying illegally where we were. He was there illegally because we were in a whites-only area, though it was perfectly legal to have black servants at the bottom of the garden in a hut. My wife and the black bishop were taken by car into the city centre. When they got out, she naturally walked at his side. He warned her not to do that, otherwise he might be arrested. On Sunday we travelled by a whites-only bus to the Anglican cathedral. Outside was a large, wonderful notice welcoming people of all races. A white priest, an Indian priest and an African priest concelebrated a mass for the congregation, which was inspiringly multi-racial. In Christ all walls come tumbling down. Afterwards there was tea for everyone, but as we left we all had to stand at separate bus stops for separate races. Nevertheless, we had seen a glorious vision. When I returned to Johannesburg in 1991, the vision was being realised. I walked towards a bus stop with a young black man. We were unsure whether he would be allowed to board the bus. It was a moment of sheer happiness when we were both accepted by the same driver, and we sat side by side for the journey together.

Israel is building a wall to keep terrorists out, but as this has sometimes meant taking land from the Palestinians to do so, it has created further Palestinian resentment. You need more than military action and a wall to combat terrorism. You have to face and deal with the injustices which promote despair and therefore terrorism. One day the Israeli wall will be demolished, as the Berlin Wall and the wall of apartheid were demolished. Can we imagine Israelis and Palestinians climbing through the ruins to hug one another? That would be another vision of the kingdom of God at last realised. However, families and churches can also build walls round themselves. Parents can inculcate a fear of what lies beyond the family boundaries. Parents can say, 'Mary and John, you must stick with people like us and then you'll be safe.'

A family with such a policy of separation keeps its members under control through fear. That type of family is very hard for a daughter-in-law or a son-in-law to join. They are told in effect, 'You can only join us if you become like us.' There is a film by Ken Loach called *Ae Fond Kiss* about a Muslim boy in Glasgow who falls for a teacher at the local Roman Catholic school. Both the Muslim and Roman Catholic communities in the film are surrounded by high defensive walls behind which people cower in fear and ignorance. When two people attempt to break down the wall, the two communities act violently to pull the lovers apart.

We all remember the poignant psalm that begins, 'By the waters of Babylon we sat down and wept when we remembered Zion (Jerusalem).' In the sixth century BCE, Babylonians conquered Judah and deported some fifty thousand Jews to Babylon. The Jews lost everything they held most dear: Jerusalem, the temple, the monarchy. Jews regarded all these features of Judah as signs of God's presence and favour. The Book of Nehemiah tells how Nehemiah, a Jewish patriot who was serving in the Persian court, heard of the dismal state of Jerusalem. After an inspection of the city at night, he roused the people to rebuild the city's defences. 'So the wall was finished.'

It wasn't just a physical wall that Nehemiah and the scribe Ezra created. There was a great debate about how to rebuild the nation. Ezra and Nehemiah argued that the nation needed a clear identity with clear blue water between the Jews and everyone else. In Ezra 10, we have a vivid and tragic scene of what we would now call racial cleansing. Ezra gathered men, women and children in the square. The people were trembling with fear. It was pouring with rain. He told them that all their foreign wives were to be deported, and so the tragic tearing apart of married people began. Ezra's and Nehemiah's policy of exclusion won.

This tragic story reminds us of those terrible scenes in Nazi Germany, as mixed marriages between Jews and Christians were broken up and Jews carried off to concentration camps. But there were powerful voices on the other side in Judaism – and we can read the vivid debate in the Old Testament. There is the book of Ruth with its story of how the great-grandmother of the ideal king, David, wasn't Jewish at all, but was descended from a mixed marriage. The book of Jonah told the story of Jonah, who was sent by God to preach to the Gentiles of Nineveh, to show that God cared for all races, not just Jews. The writer of Isaiah 56 declared that foreigners and eunuchs should be included as full members of God's people and be allowed to worship in the temple, if they do justice and keep the Sabbath, 'for my house shall be called a house of prayer for all peoples' (56:7). Jesus quoted this in Mark 11:17, for he preached inclusion like Ruth, Jonah and the latter part of Isaiah.

We've also had Ezras and Nehemiahs in the history of the church as rigorists and excluders. In the early church some Christians gave way under persecution and torture. The rigorists said that they were not prepared to include them in the church. The church must be pure. Others contended that the church was for sinners and that the Gospel offered forgiveness and new beginnings. Fortunately they prevailed and the church remained catholic – for everyone. After the Reformation we had more Ezras and Nehemiahs who were determined to build excluding walls. They said that membership of the church by baptism was indiscriminate; it let in some very doubtful people. Only those who had a specific type of conversion experience could be members. Today we have some vocal Ezras and Nehemiahs in the Anglican Communion. There are those who wish to exclude half the human race from being priests or bishops. They want a church with walls to keep women out of ordained ministry. Pope John Paul II forbade even any discussion of the ordination of women. Others want to build walls to keep all gay women and men out. On the other hand, some liberal Christians would like to build walls to exclude all conservatives.

When I first travelled across Europe in the 1950s there were many frontiers: crossing a frontier was a serious business. The armed guards came onto the train – it was always particularly alarming in the middle of the night when the train had to stop at some isolated station. Now, thanks to the European Union, one can sweep through without stopping. On the roads, you pass from France to Belgium to Germany, to Italy, and see the deserted frontier posts as you go; yet Italians, French, Germans, and Belgians remain just as distinct as they ever were. This demonstrates vividly how we can have difference without division, difference without high walls to keep some people in and other people out. Moreover, interaction between different peoples and outlooks is enriching. The Old Testament took the creation and flood stories and some psalms from other religions and cultures. Christians don't agree about the possession of nuclear weapons. Why then does it matter if we don't agree about all ethical questions about sex?

'Love one another,' says Jesus in the second lesson (John 15:12). Love and friendship break down high walls and leap across barriers. We can be friends with people with whom we disagree and friends with those who are very different from ourselves. In our churches and in our individual lives, let us examine ourselves as to whether we have built walls and sought to expel those from our hearts and groups just because they are different from ourselves.

# 40.

# Wrestling Jacob

Isaac and Rebekah had twin sons, Esau the first born and Jacob. Tonight's first lesson from Genesis 32 tells two stories. The first is about the approaching reconciliation of the twin brothers after many years of hatred and suspicion. The second story is about the mysterious stranger with whom Jacob wrestled all night. Was it God himself or his representative? We sang as our first hymn one of Charles Wesley's most memorable hymns:

> Come, O thou Traveller unknown,
> Whom still I hold, but cannot see;
> My company before is gone.
> And I am left alone with thee;
> With thee all night I mean to stay
> And wrestle till the break of day.

*NEH 350*

Esau and Jacob had been rivals from early days. Jacob tricked Esau and stole his rights as the first born. Jacob tricked his father, Isaac, into giving him the blessing reserved for the first born. As a result Jacob was given fertile land, while Esau was given a stony area, dry and difficult to cultivate. Naturally, this made Esau very angry with his brother Jacob, so Jacob left home and went to stay with his uncle. However, when Jacob reached his uncle, Jacob the deceiver was in his turn tricked. His uncle tricked him into working for fourteen years in return for the right to marry his uncle's two daughters.

By the time Jacob left his uncle, he was a wealthy man with large flocks, two wives and two slave girls as his mistresses. Now he had to face his angry brother, who appeared with a large band of men. In tonight's lesson from Genesis 32, Jacob sends a message of reconciliation and offers a substantial gift to Esau. In the next chapter we hear of how touchingly they were reconciled after many years of enmity. 'Esau ran to meet him, and embraced him, and fell on his neck and kissed him, and they wept.' (Genesis 33:4.) But before that Jacob comes to the crucial turning point of his life. 'Jacob was left alone, and a man wrestled with him until daybreak.' (32:24.) Hitherto Jacob had been successful through being a crook and a trickster. Now he is confronted with the fact that he has been deceiving not just Esau his brother, but God himself. He'd gained his father's blessing through trickery. He now gains a blessing from God by having the courage to wrestle with God, and his name is changed. Let us note three features of this story.

1. Jacob's thigh is dislocated in the struggle. Encounters with God are always disturbing and in every way dislocating. When Isaiah had a vision of God in the temple he reacted 'Woe is me! I am lost, for I am a man of unclean lips, and I live among a people of unclean lips; yet my eyes have seen the king, the Lord of hosts!' When Peter experienced the ability of Jesus to locate the fish in the lake, Peter fell at his feet, 'Go away from me, Lord, for I am a sinful man!' (Luke 5:8.) We note that God seems often to find it easier to work through a person with gaping holes and huge faults than through someone complacent and impenetrable: Abraham who left his father; Jacob the deceiver; Moses the murderer; David the adulterer; Peter who denied knowing Jesus.

2. His name is changed by God from Jacob meaning one who gains an advantage by deceit and trickery. Jacob becomes Israel – that name means the one who strives, wrestles with God and prevails. As we have seen, his changed character is represented by his change of name, and this makes possible his reconciliation with his brother. The name Israel becomes the name of the nation and was taken by the revived nation in 1948. God wants us to stand up to him. We should not expect faith to be easy, we should expect to have to struggle and wrestle. One of the great features of the psalms is that the writers wrestle with God in their distress and anger. 'O God, wherefore art thou absent from us so long: why is thy wrath so hot against the people of thy pasture?' (Psalm 74:1.) Rowan Williams sees this story of wrestling Jacob as a parable of how we should read Scripture. He says that we shall receive God's blessing from it only when we wrestle with it; the blessing will come when we cease to expect it to be like an oracle dropped down from heaven: 'scripture is the record of an encounter and a contest' (*Open to Judgement*, 28).

3.  Jacob asks God's name but he receives no reply. In the Bible
    a name is not just a label but the way into a person's inner
    being. To know the name is to have control over that person.
    Remember how later Moses (Exodus 3:13) asks God to tell
    him his name; he needs it because the people will ask him what
    it is. God replies: 'I am who I am.' That was a very ambiguous
    reply. Some believe that God really meant, 'mind your own
    business'. It is also sometimes translated as 'I will be what I
    will be.' On another occasion, Moses asks God: 'Show me your
    glory, I pray.' God reminds Moses that no one can see God and
    live and offers an ingenious solution: '[W]hile my glory passes
    by I will put you in a cleft of the rock, and I will cover you with
    my hand until I have passed by, then I will take away my hand,
    and you will be able to see my back; but my face shall not be
    seen.' (Exodus 33:18-23.)

Often when we are trying to pray, we encounter a cloud, a darkness, an
emptiness, for we cannot capture God, we cannot put him to our own
uses. God is not another being but, as it were, a lot 'larger' than we are.
We must realise that God is quite other. 'I am who I am.' Ponder then
this encounter between God and Jacob: the dislocation of the thigh; the
change of name and nature; the refusal of God to disclose his name.
Sooner or later we are going to have an experience similar to that which
Jacob had at Jabbok.

Charles Raven was a memorable First World War chaplain and later
Vice-Chancellor of Cambridge University. He sailed over to France in
1917 to join his regiment. On his first night he felt the necessity to face
the possibility of his own death or injury:

> when death looked me in the face, my manhood withered and
> collapsed. For what seemed hours I was in an agony of fear . . . and
> suddenly as if spoken in the very room His words 'For their sakes
> I consecrate myself' . . . for the next nine months He was never
> absent, and I never alone. . . . He . . . was with me when blown
> up by a shell, and gassed, and sniped at, with me in hours of
> bombardment and the daily walk of death. . . .
>
> *Charles Raven,* A Wanderer's Way, *157*

I think also of someone I know going through a totally different kind of
wrestling at the ford of Jabbok. He was a well-known scholar, a former
professor whose whole identity and purpose in life had been expressed
through his scholarship and huge collection of books. When he was

more than eighty, he had to sell nearly all his books and move out of a large and elegant house. Selling virtually all his books made him feel naked and unprotected, just an ordinary person without any distinctive features. It was as though he asked himself: 'If I lose all my books who will I be?'

Others face the loss of a simple faith based on a literal reading of the Bible. They discover painfully that the Bible is complex and often contradictory. Perhaps they wrestle with such a question as this: when people talk about a return to biblical values, do they mean someone like Jacob with two wives and two slaves who are also his mistresses? They go through a period of wrestling and discover that though God will not give us his name, he does give us his blessing; they discover that our faith should be in him, not in any book, however important. Are you wrestling with God about anything at the moment? Or do you think that the idea of wrestling with God is totally wrong?

# 41.

# Ordained Fifty Years

I was ordained deacon in St Paul's Cathedral, London, fifty years ago in 1959 on this Feast of St Michael and All Angels. I'm celebrating my deaconing as well as my forty-nine years as a priest. For all priestly ministry should be as a deacon, which means 'servant'. We remember the saying of Jesus: 'The Son of Man came not to be served but to serve.' (Matthew 20:28.) My first reaction to this anniversary is to pray 'Lord have mercy' in penitence and 'Thanks be to God' in gratitude, not least for the twenty-one years that Portsmouth Cathedral has been our home. All the hymns I have chosen have a particular significance to me. 'Christ the fair glory of the holy angels' was the hymn with which we processed into St Paul's Cathedral for the ordination. The second hymn, 'God everlasting', was suddenly produced by my vicar when I was a curate; he said he'd written it especially for that Sunday but I suspect he'd had it in his drawer for some time. In the final hymn, 'Forth in the peace of Christ we go', we have the phrase 'We are the church'. We shall all sing that, for you are just as much the church as I am. We'll know the whole body of the church is coming alive when lay people start celebrating the anniversaries of their baptism and confirmation. That is why I have chosen today to meditate on three remarks made to me not by other clergy but by laypeople.

The first story took place in the late 1950s, when I was a curate in a slum parish in London. We wore our cassocks in the street and were called 'Father'. Soon after I was ordained, I was walking down the street. Two little boys were playing near a house. One looked up at me and said to his friend, 'Look, there's Gawd.' His friend replied: 'Don't be stupid. It's only Farver.' Were they poking fun at me because I looked self-important in my new cassock? Or was the boy saying that in some way I reminded him of God? But the other boy was also right. It was only 'Farver'. St Paul wrote that we have only earthenware pots to contain the treasures of God (2 Corinthians 4:7).

A woman priest was once asked 'What was your most important theological and spiritual experience?' She replied, 'The birth of my three children.' She saw this ordinary human event from the Godward side. 'Look, there's Gawd,' said one boy. The other replied, 'It's only Farver.' Was the divine being mediated through a human being, the divine treasure in an earthenware jar? An old Mirfield Father once told me that the evening of his ordination, after his first day in black, he gingerly pulled up his trousers to see whether his legs had gone black too. In Jesus, God was mediated through an ordinary human life. Jesus was not ordained; he held no ecclesiastical office.

The second story I want to tell you happened in the 1960s when I became vicar of a country parish. One day I visited an old man who was dying in his cottage. I asked him if he would like to receive Communion before he died. 'Yes,' he said eagerly, but then added, 'but I've never been confirmed.' I explained that since he really wished to receive Communion before he died, he could do so without being confirmed. The next day I took bread and wine, cup and plate, and celebrated the Eucharist by his bed. Afterwards, he said, 'That was wonderful, vicar. I always thought Communion was reserved for the gentry.' That was said in 1968, not 1868, and in a village within sight of Bristol, which had been served by above-average priests, and really cared for by the gentry in their manor house, who rebuilt cottages and church.

The Church of England over the centuries has done an immense amount for the poor but only in rare places like St Agatha's in Portsmouth have we been a church of the poor. We once visited Sandringham parish church. An attempt had been made to make the visitors feel at home. There was a large lighted candle and a book in which you could write your prayers. But the royal pews and silver altar spoke a different message. The young couple in front of us heard that unspoken message and commented, 'It's not for people like us.' Is that what people say when they come into our churches and cathedrals? 'It's not for people like us.' What a damning verdict. What can we do to put such ideas to flight?

In the 1920s there was a debate about creating a new diocese of Portsmouth. Influential people argued that Portsmouth was unsuitable for a diocese. Portsmouth was no place for a cathedral. It was too poor and too run-down. Such people obviously thought the church was for the well-off, not for the poor. 'It's not for people like us,' the couple said about Sandringham church. The old man thought Communion was reserved for the gentry.

The third story I want to pass on happened in the 1980s. I was vicar of three remote parishes in north Yorkshire, on the edge of the Dales. One parish had its church set in a lawn area used for burying ashes, but no memorial stones or graves. One had a church set in a traditional churchyard. The third parish had a churchyard but no church. To have a churchyard but no church suited those whose main attachment was to the graves of their relations. For its upkeep they somewhat incongruously but enthusiastically held clay pigeon shoots and dinner dances. One of the parishioners there once remarked to me about the parish which had a church but only a lawn for burying ashes: 'You know, that church is not a proper church.' 'Why?' I asked. He replied: 'Because it has no churchyard.' He assumed that the church is there to have a churchyard beside it, and that the churchyard is more important than the church building. He felt that the purpose of the church was to help us to cope with death and whatever lies beyond, and to cherish memories.

The church is here for more than that. It is here to inspire and care for the lives of the present population, to gather them together in the Eucharist where we experience how the material world matters to God so much that his Son gives himself through it. Yet the Eucharist is also celebrated with angels, archangels and the whole company of heaven. It takes us into the heavenly places. Sadly, when a competition was held for great Britons, no one suggested St Richard of Chichester, St Thomas of Canterbury, George Herbert, Josephine Butler, Bishop George Bell or Portsmouth's Father Dolling of St Agatha's. In a place like Portsmouth, Nelson is widely remembered. But how many other people from the past are? For the past is very past in the United Kingdom.

A group of teenagers was taken by their teacher into their ancient parish church. When he told them how old it was and how many generations of people, now dead, filled the pews where they were now sitting, the youngsters expressed their unease, even fear, with a shivering sound. They felt at ease only with the immediately contemporary. The past was unreal and irrelevant, or only populated by frightening ghosts. They had no experience of the way in which, as we have seen, the Eucharist unites past and present. In my parishes, an older generation was at ease with saying that a church without a churchyard was not a proper church. Though this represents only a partial view of the church, it contains a vital perspective, rare today. I would urge us to believe that we are not a church if we neglect the Last Things and the Communion of Saints. As we sang in the first hymn:

> May the blest Mother of our God and Saviour,
> May the assembly of the saints in glory
> May the celestial companies of angels
> Ever assist us.

*NEH 190*

We are not a proper church if we cannot echo the words of St Augustine at the end of *The City of God* as he looked forward to the life of heaven: 'There we shall be still and see; we shall see and we shall love; we shall love and we shall praise. Behold what will be, in the end, without end! For what is our end but to reach that kingdom which has no end!'

# 42.

# Sacramental Christianity

John the Baptist said to the crowds coming for baptism, 'I baptise you with water' (Matthew 3:11).

I once had a university student from the Far East who insisted that Christian baptism had nothing to do with water. Baptism, he thought, was about individual faith. Water was irrelevant. I think he'd been influenced by both extreme Protestant groups and Eastern religions. Both regard the spiritual and material as enemies. It's a simple solution to life: divide it into two parts. All good things are spiritual. All bad things are material. However, as Archbishop William Temple insisted: 'Christianity is the most materialistic of all great religions' (*Readings in St John's Gospel,* xxiv).

For many that will be an outrageous statement. Why should it be outrageous? After all, Christianity starts with the belief that God created the material world. How did God communicate with the Jews? Through flesh and blood priests and prophets; through their worship which used material things like goats and incense, and, increasingly, through writings. We believe above all that God communicated with us not through a message or a book but through a person, the Word made flesh, Jesus. We believe that he was born of an earthly mother who had borne him in her womb for nine months, then held him in her arms. We believe that God communicates with us through the seven sacramental ministries of baptism, confirmation, Eucharist, confession, anointing, ordination, marriage. The Revised Catechism of 1962 offered this definition of a sacrament: 'the use of material things as signs and pledges of God's grace and as a means by which we receive his gifts. The two parts of a sacrament are the outward and visible sign, and the inward and spiritual grace.' We also believe that God communicates with us through what are sometimes called sacramentals, such as Scripture, music, voices, instruments, paintings, candles, vestments, stained glass, incense, icons, the sign of the cross.

How did Jesus become a member of John's community, which was preparing for the Messiah? By offering John the Baptist some serious thoughts? No, through a ritual action, by baptism with water. In his own ministry, Jesus himself constantly used material things through which to convey grace and truth – by feedings in the wilderness and after the resurrection at the lake side, in the upper room in a house in Emmaus. He healed by laying on of hands and sometimes by mixing mud with his own spit – you can't get more physical than that (John 9:6). At the Last Supper he promised that in the future he would be present through the material things of bread and wine. In the early church we see the same use of material things for spiritual purposes.

In today's lesson from Acts 8, Peter and John laid hands on some Samaritans who had been baptised, and through those hands they received the Holy Spirit. If the universe is a sacrament of God, if the material things are capable of being used for spiritual purposes, then how we use the material world matters to God – how we use our bodies, how we use our cars, how we plan our towns, whether we respect the atmosphere, whether we care about global warming. John brought Jesus into his group by a ritual washing.

It is interesting what sort of adjectives are commonly attached to the word 'ritual' – 'meaningless' ritual, 'out of date' ritual, 'mere' ritual. Rituals can be life-enhancing, precious, life-giving. One of my grandsons has just celebrated his third birthday. He had a cake with candles and blew them out. 'But of course,' you say. Try saying to a child: 'We're not going to have presents or a birthday cake with enough candles to show your age, it's a meaningless ritual. Instead we'll just stand around and think nice thoughts about you. Or perhaps have quiche lorraine.' If you take away the familiar shared ritual of the birthday cake, the lighting of the candles, and the blowing them out, then all continuity is lost and all sense of solidarity with previous birthdays or other peoples' birthdays. The same is true of adults: try saying to your husband, your wife, or your best friend 'I know it's your birthday, but you're such a spiritual person that a present would be far too crude, so I've brought you a loving thought.' Why do we need sacraments, sacramentals, material things and rituals that convey what words alone cannot? Because we're not just minds with legs. We're psychosomatic people – our spirit and body entwined in an inextricable unity. We express ourselves through our bodies, our smiles, our hugs, our frowns, and our sexuality.

It's common now to talk about 'body language'. What a revealing phrase that is: body language. Our bodies convey messages children's games and rituals go back centuries, some go back for two thousand years or more. Christian sacraments also have long histories – and much of that history is pre-Christian. From earliest times, long before Judaism, water was used for ritual purification. Converts to Judaism were baptised. Jews purify themselves with water. Muslims are fascinated when they come into the cathedral and see the holy water stoups at the doors to remind us of our baptism and when they see the font full of water. Someone converting to Islam has to take a ritual bath. Before prayers a Muslim has to wash their hands, wrists, mouth, nose, face, arms and feet.

A Jewish woman attended the Eucharist for the first time. She said to me, 'How Jewish it all is: the thanksgivings, the blessings over the bread and wine.' In fact, its roots go further back still. Three thousand years ago when the Jews were conquering Canaan, they found that the people celebrated a spring festival. A family group would take the first lamb up to the top of the local hill, slit its throat, and pour out the life blood on the altar. They prayed for fertility in the land, in the family and among the animals; then they would roast and then eat together the sacrificed lamb. When the choir sing the prayer 'Lamb of God you take away the sin of the world', I sometimes think of that family struggling up the hill, taking their lamb to be sacrificed, roasted and fed upon. All that went into the Jewish Passover, which went in turn into the Eucharist. So, too, did the laying on of hands in confirmation, ordination and healing, the use of oil at baptism, confirmation, for healing and ordination. All these have long Jewish roots and even deeper roots as well, ones that go far back into the earliest days of human history.

When John baptised Jesus he was not only pointing ahead to Christian baptism, he was drawing upon a long tradition of the use of water in religion that stretched back to the beginning of time. Are we grateful that in the sacraments and sacramentals, God shows us how material things can be dependable means of grace and truth? Can we be grateful that the sacraments are rooted in many thousands of years of human faith and experience? Can we be grateful to God for using material things as ladders let down from heaven?

# 43.

# Increase Our Faith

From this morning's Gospel: 'The apostles said to the Lord: Increase our faith.' (Luke 17:5.) Do you want to increase, deepen, strengthen your faith? In today's epistle, Paul speaks of Timothy's faith and how he received it from his grandmother and mother (2 Timothy 1:1-14). Our own personal faith often catches fire from the faith of others, hence the importance of getting to know the saints and catching their faith. Think how people have been moved to sacrificial action by the faith of St Francis, whom the church celebrates on Monday.

'Lord, increase our faith,' the apostles asked Jesus. I want to suggest two ways in which the Lord can and does increase our faith. Look at the world with wonder; share the faith and trust that Jesus had in his Father.

*1.*

In a Trinity Sunday sermon, John Henry Newman said that 'a religious mind is ever marvelling'. The more we get to know about the world, the universe, the more we should marvel. Recall Psalm 8, 'When I consider your heavens the work of your fingers, the moon and the stars that you have ordained.' 'When I consider': considering, turning something over in your imagination. This is an important aspect of prayer. Modern science enables us to do just that. The Hubble Space Telescope has received light that has been streaking through space for thirteen billion years, when the universe was only five per cent of its present age. Consider that and marvel.

On Southsea Common there was for a short time a model dinosaur. It didn't last long. We have a good idea why that dinosaur disappeared. But why did the original dinosaurs disappear? Probably they were destroyed by a huge meteorite which hit the earth sixty-five million years ago. What a profound disappointment to modern boys and girls. The choirboys might like the idea of a dinosaur larger than the cathedral lurking in the next street, but it would certainly have wanted to gobble them all up. Another strange fact about our universe is its delicate balance. An eminent British physicist wrote a few years ago that the more he examined the universe, the more evidence he found that in some sense it knew we humans were coming. That is to say, that the laws of the universe are so very precise that the slightest variation in this or that feature would have prevented human life ever evolving.

Let us move down the scale from the vast to the small, down to the mystery of migrating birds like the sandpipers. Sandpipers each year fly nine thousand miles from the southern tip of South America to the frozen islands of northern Canada and back again. Each year they know exactly when to set out: at the time that the horseshoe crabs are laying their eggs which will nourish the birds on their journey. Each bird begins life as a single fertilised cell. Each microscopic cell contains the equivalent of a set of maps, a compass, a sextant and something like a satellite navigational system.

I'm not saying all this proves that there is a God, but remember Newman's phrase about how the religious mind is forever marvelling. Facts about the universe or a tiny bird's migratory skills do suggest that there is much more to the universe than meets the eye. Isn't it odd that our minds should be capable of understanding the universe – does this suggest that the universe is also the product of a mind?

'Increase our faith,' said the apostles. When we contemplate the universe, are we not moved to wonder and gratitude? 'Heaven and earth are full of thy glory', we sing in the Sanctus. But we are also bewildered at the immense amount of suffering caused by natural disasters or disease. We ask 'Why is there so much suffering?' We must also ask 'Why do we also have art, beauty, love, and gratitude?' There is cancer but also Mozart; war but also the baby at the breast.

There is an odd instinct to be grateful for life. 'I'm so thankful,' people say. A novelist once climbed a mountain. At the top she gazed at the scene, moved by its beauty. She wanted to say 'Thank you'. But she was an agnostic; there was no one to say thank you to.

'Increase our faith,' asked the apostles. Does investigating the universe do that? It may well move us to admire the intelligence behind it that is ceaselessly at work and to be awed by the power and scale of it all. But can we find a face behind it? Or do we have to look elsewhere for that?

## 2.

If we draw near to Jesus does that increase our faith? I remember climbing a mountain some years ago. The path led up through trees. For much of the climb, the view was obscured by dense trees. But from time to time there was a clearing and we had a glimpse of part of the view. After a long climb, we finally reached the summit. The trees dropped away and we could see the whole view all around.

I used to teach world religions for Open University. The more I got to know major world faiths, the more I became fascinated by and grateful for the truths and insights of Hinduism, Buddhism, Judaism and Islam. At the same time I saw even more clearly the uniqueness of Jesus, as the word of God made flesh, as a human being transparent to God, through whom God uniquely acted. It was like that climb on the mountain on the way up, where there were glimpses of part of the view from clearings. It was only at the mountain top that I could see the whole view all around.

I think of the compassion of Jesus for the prodigal son; his compassion for all sorts of outcasts, his compassion for his mother as he hung on the cross. I think of that verse in the Gospels: when Jesus 'saw a great crowd, he had great compassion for them, because they were like sheep without a shepherd' (Mark 6:34). Yet Jesus was also tough and courageous, challenging people through his actions and words, though he knew it would probably lead to his death. God is revealed in loving care for those in desperate need; revealed in the suffering and struggle of Jesus in the garden of and on the cross. God's vindication of the way of Jesus is in the resurrection.

We say at the end of prayers 'through Jesus Christ our Lord', but do we really mean it? What does it mean in our Eucharistic prayers when we say Jesus is the one 'in whom all our hungers are satisfied'? We are moved to marvel by contemplating and investigating the world, but we are moved to worship and prayer when we approach God through Jesus, through his faith in God. He takes us to the Father through the Spirit, we share his faith, for we are in him by baptism and nourished by him in the Eucharist.

# 44.
# Praying

'Almighty God, you have made us for yourself, and our hearts are restless till they find their rest in you.' Those are familiar words from St Augustine's *Confessions,* written 397-8 CE, but also now used as the opening words of the collect for today, Trinity XVII. We often hear the invitation 'Let us pray'. But do we? In a book recently I came across the phrase 'contemporary prayerless Christianity'. The writer was deploring our failure to help a thirsty generation of young people to share in the riches of the Christian spiritual tradition. As I came out of Portsmouth cathedral the other evening a couple appeared at the door. I asked, 'Are you wanting to look round?' 'No,' the man responded in a foreign accent. 'I want to pray.' I might have guessed he wasn't English. English visitors eagerly ask about some naval monument but rarely ask for a quiet place to pray.

It's true of other cathedrals, too, where chapels for prayer are not used as much as they should be, though now we have stands where people can light candles and that is very popular. It is marvellously inspiring to go into a church or cathedral and see a whole bank of lighted candles, each one representing a prayer offered, however uncertainly, or a longing or an act of penitence. Are most of the English embarrassed by people at prayer, by people who take religion seriously? Is lighting a candle more neutral, more acceptable? Lighting candles in church is more acceptable, perhaps, because we also light candles on birthday cakes! The great Victorian architect, Loughborough Pearson, who built Truro Cathedral, said that he designed churches to bring people to their knees. I once visited a remote church on the Norfolk coast, attracted by its architecture. To my surprise, it was the gate to heaven. I knelt there for half an hour or more, and time stopped. I felt God holding me in his hand.

A new Roman Catholic website has been created for people to exchange horror stories about noisy chatter in church. There's even a T shirt to wear in church inscribed 'Shh, I'm praying' to ensure the wearer is not disturbed. Are English Christians like people on a walk who are always pausing for stops on the way, so they never reach their destination? It is easy to get so caught up with maintaining institutions that we forget that our destination is God. Is it that we know a few prayers to say but don't know how to pray? Are we reluctant to pray because we fear getting near to God in case he should ask more from us than we are willing to give? Or are we like a man I met years ago who said: 'I prayed my mother should not die. She did die and I've never prayed since.'

What do we mean by prayer? Many people only pray when they want something. That is a curious kind of relationship. Do you only get in touch with a friend when you want to borrow money? Prayer is basically attention to God: trying to attend to him with every faculty we have.

I want to suggest three ways of praying based on the letters TLC – better known as, 'tender loving care'. I'm going to use these three letters to remind us of 'thanksgiving, liturgy and contemplation'.

## *T for Thanks*

There is nothing like gratitude for breaking down barriers and building bridges between people. We know that if ever we feel someone is distant, gratitude bridges that distance and breaks down reserve. That is, when we say something like 'I am so grateful for your friendship'; or 'I'm grateful for what you said the other day'; or what every parent longs to hear: 'You've always been a lovely mum/dad to me.' If you want to make a fresh start in prayer, (and all of us need to do that from time to time) gratitude is a good place to begin. In the evening go over the day: remember the people and things you've enjoyed – the particularly kind assistant at the supermarket, the cathedral in the evening sunlight, the scrumptious meal prepared by a friend, the warm welcome from your dog when you got home, or the wonderful gift of prayer.

Remember the General Thanksgiving, 'We bless thee for our creation, preservation, and all the blessings of this life; but above all for . . . Jesus Christ, for the means of grace and the hope of glory.' What a marvellous list.

## *L for Liturgy*

By that title, I refer to both praying the liturgy and using the liturgy in our own prayers. We once watched the film *The Madness of King George*. When the doctors were administering very painful therapy for his mental illness, he cried out and prayed to 'Almighty God unto whom all hearts be open' from the Eucharist; 'Almighty and most merciful Father, we have erred and strayed from thy ways like lost sheep' from Morning and Evening Prayer. The Lord's Prayer is an obvious gift to use in this way. Pray it very slowly, clause by clause and let each phrase rest on your tongue like a lozenge. Allow it to dissolve slowly on the tongue.

There is a moving CD made by students at Westcott House Theological College, Cambridge called 'Glimpses of God'. One ordinand tells how the family had gone to take the coffin containing his uncle to the church to rest there overnight. His nephew stayed behind to watch for a while. As he did so he felt the Sanctus, 'Holy Holy Holy' from the Eucharist rise in his heart and mind and take him over, lifting him up into the great chorus of praise from all creation.

There are also themes and phrases from the readings we can take into our personal prayers. Think for example about that very memorable story from Genesis 2 this morning. The man sees the woman for the first time and exclaims in delight, 'This is at last bone of my bone and flesh of my flesh.' We might ponder being alone, loneliness, and ask, 'Who completes me?' Or we might turn to today's Gospel from St Mark (10:2-16) and ask 'What could strengthen marriage?' 'Am I ready to share the pain and desperate disappointment of those whose marriages are breaking down?'

We should also try to pray the liturgy, so that we're not just hearing words but praying them as we hear them. During the Kyries, we should feel a deep sense of penitence for our sins and the sins of the world. We can turn the creed into a joyful celebration of God's great acts, especially if we could sing it as once was the custom. We can treat the Agnus Dei as a heartfelt cry for peace. At Evensong, as we hear the Magnificat, we can express a great outpouring of gratitude to Mary and for Mary.

## C for Contemplation

We must move beyond thinking about stories; move beyond lots of words to focus on just one or two words, or an object like a lit candle, an icon. The fourteenth century anonymous author of *The Cloud of Unknowing* described this kind of prayer as 'blind loving of God'. Not thinking anything, not picturing anything, just hanging onto some simple phrase like 'Our Father' repeated again and again as often as we need to keep our attention focussed. Focussed on what, focussed on whom? Focus on the cloud of unknowing.

Recall Psalm 42: 'My soul is athirst for God, yea, even for the living God.' Go on repeating it slowly. Don't worry if you can only say it half-heartedly. The author of *The Cloud of Unknowing* wrote: 'Strike that thick cloud of unknowing with the sharp dart of longing love, and on no account whatever think of giving up.' One great benefit of this type of prayer is that we have to abandon any sense that we have got God taped, that we can control him for our own purposes or command him to give us warm comfort. We realise that really we know very little of God: what matters is that he knows us through and through. Ponder Psalm 139, 'O Lord, thou hast searched me out and known me ... lo, there is not a word in my tongue but thou, O Lord, knowest it altogether.'

The chief aim of contemplative prayer is expressed in a verse of Psalm 46: 'Be still then, and know that I am God.' *The Cloud of Unknowing* says 'Lift up your heart to God with humble love; and mean God himself and not what you get out of him.' This is how we learn self-less loving. We learn to pray to be still and attentive for God's sake alone. Such prayer can seem a struggle, so sometimes we don't realise we have been praying until we stop.

TLC means this: a prayer of gratitude; praying the liturgy and using its texts in our own prayer; learning to be still and contemplate. 'Be still before the Lord, and wait patiently for him' (Psalm 37). The saintly Archbishop Michael Ramsey called his last book on prayer *Be Still and Know*. That is it. Be still and know.

We pray in today's collect: 'Almighty God, you have made us for yourself, and our hearts are restless till they find their rest in you: pour your love into our hearts and draw us to yourself, and so bring us at last to your heavenly city where we shall see you face to face; through Jesus Christ our Lord.'

# 45.

# The Silence of God

O that you would tear open the heavens and come down, so that the mountains would quake at your presence.

*Isaiah 64:1*

We don't know the precise context of tonight's first lesson from Isaiah 64. Probably it was written after the exile of Jews in Babylon. They returned from around 538 BCE. Perhaps the Temple which meant so much them had not yet been rebuilt. Was Isaiah exasperated by the decline of faith and vision? But whatever the historical context, Isaiah expressed a universal cry of anguish. A cry of anguish which we have uttered in some form at some time. 'God do something, act, show yourself.' As Psalm 44 puts it: 'Up, Lord, why sleepest thou?' or more bluntly 'For heaven's sake, God, wake up, get out of bed and do something.' In the Old Testament, Jews often argued with God, expressed doubts and frustration. The angel of the Lord appeared to Gideon and addressed him, 'The Lord is with you, you mighty man of valour.' Gideon, however, wasn't going to be taken in by that sort of flannel. He demanded to know from the angel why so many terrible things had happened to them if the Lord was on their side. Our fathers go on talking about what wonderful things God has done in the past. But where is he now? (Judges 6.)

'Lamb of God,' we pray, 'you take away the sin of the world, grant us peace.' 'But does he? Where is the evidence?' Sometimes the music for the Agnus Dei makes this an unbearably agonising cry. Christians say: 'But God has intervened through Jesus.' Jews reply, 'Jesus cannot be the Messiah, because since his time the world hasn't changed. If he had been the Messiah, his coming would have inaugurated universal peace and justice, what we call shalom.' How do we Christians respond to that?

The Jews themselves have a lot of jokes about their long experience of exile, deportation and persecution. Often the jokes are a form of a continuous argument with God about the injustices of life and the silence and inactivity of God. Rabbi Lionel Blue tells the story of a man who experienced every form of disaster. His wife left him, his children turned against him, he lost all his money. One morning, in the depths of despair, he was having his breakfast. He was just about to eat a piece of toast when it dropped on the floor. It seemed like the last straw. But, lo and behold, it had fallen with the buttered side up! He went to see his rabbi and told him what had happened. 'Do you think God is at last being kind to me again?' 'No,' said the rabbi. 'You just buttered the wrong side of the toast.'

When it comes to talking about the Holocaust, the traditional explanations for evil and suffering die on Jewish lips. Yes, they had sinned, but they could not believe that their sins were so great that God would allow a third of all Jews to be brutally killed. Some Jews contended that the Holocaust was God's way of purifying the Jews to prepare them for the creation of Israel and the coming of the Messiah. One wrote, 'No theological statement should be made that could not be made in the presence of burning children.' For other Jews, after the Holocaust, God simply became unbelievable. In his short story 'Yosl Rakover Talks to God', Zvi Kolitz joined the long Jewish tradition of arguing with God (Genesis 18 and 32; Job; many Psalms): 'I should like You to tell me whether there is any sin in the world deserving of such a punishment as the punishment we have received? . . . I should like to ask You, O Lord – and this question burns in me like a consuming fire – what more, O, what more must transpire before You unveil Your countenance again to the world? . . . We have the right to know what are the limits of Your forbearance?'

Stories are more eloquent than abstractions. There is a story that one afternoon in a German death camp, a group of Jews assembled in one hut to put God on trial for having abandoned his chosen people to cruelty and death. The case for the prosecution was overwhelming. At the end, one by one they gave their verdict: 'Guilty', 'Guilty', 'Guilty'. Then there was a deep silence. After a long while, someone said, 'Nevertheless, it is time for prayers,' and they prayed. There is the astonishing paradox. God guilty, God unbelievable, God silent, God apparently impotent, God apparently uncaring. 'Nevertheless, we must pray.'

Some Christians have a sanguine belief that God will always deliver us from anything too awful. A few years ago a bishop said in this cathedral during an address to the clergy that God would act to prevent human beings destroying the world, for example, by nuclear weapons. It is a comforting thought. But was he right? Sixty-five million years ago, give or take a few hundred years, it seems likely that an asteroid six miles in diameter collided with the earth. It is thought that a basin one hundred and ten miles across in Mexico is where it landed. Three years of total dust and darkness resulted and half of all living things died. Why didn't God prevent that? Why didn't he rend the heavens and come down, as Isaiah put it in the first lesson?

We must be honest, and say we don't know. We trust that history is like a detective story: all will be revealed in the last chapter. Then we will look back and see all sorts of clues that we missed at the time. We can also say, in light of Advent and Christmas, that when God does come down and act, it is all very humble, vulnerable and low-profile. After all, the baby could have miscarried, or been trampled by the ox or the ass. Like a parent, God gives us freedom; otherwise we would never grow up. We parents can all think back to occasions when we gave permission and the result was awful. When God created, he limited his freedom to act, limited his scope to intervene dramatically. At every point in every decision, he can nudge us, try to influence us, but never so overwhelmingly that we cease to be free to say 'No'.

Henri Nouwen, a remarkable and troubled Dutch Roman Catholic priest, died in 1996. Many have studied his book *The Return of the Prodigal* in groups. Michael Ford recounted in his biography of him, *Wounded Prophet: A Portrait of Henri J.M. Nouwen* (39), how a few months before he died, he developed a fascination with trapeze artists. He was fascinated by seeing them fly through the air to be caught by another they trusted. For him that was a parable of faith. He wanted to try it out, to experience it for himself. Everyone was flabbergasted, because Nouwen was extraordinarily clumsy. He was hardly capable of making a cup of coffee. After washing up, he naturally dried the things, but he often absentmindedly put the utensils back into the washing-up water. Yet in his sixties he was determined to risk everything. One day he climbed up the ladder, put on his safety harness and swung ever higher on a trapeze. 'I can only fly freely when I know there is a catcher to catch me,' he said. 'Trust the catcher' became his watchword as priest and teacher. He had taken the ultimate risk and experienced the ultimate assurance. 'Dying is trusting in the catcher,' he said.

The churches have never faced up to the fact that over many centuries, they allowed the development of Christian anti-Semitism. Most continental Christians publicly witnessed what was happening to Jews during the war – how they were persecuted, arrested and deported. What happened to them after that was more widely known in Europe than was ever admitted. In Britain, Archbishop William Temple knew, for in the House of Lords in March 1943 he passionately condemned the systematic slaughter of Jews in Germany. The silence of churches about the Holocaust is as taxing to faith as the silence of God. Should we try to share the paradoxical faith of those Jews in the camp who, having found God guilty, responded: 'Nevertheless we must pray'?

# 46.
# Tradition and Innovation

Sixty-four years ago, my two years of national service were drawing to an end. I was preparing to go up to Cambridge. My college had been founded nearly five hundred years before I arrived. I was constantly reminded of the long and rich tradition I was privileged to share. At dinner in halls in the evening, portraits of notable past members looked down upon us and seemed to say, 'Welcome to our great tradition.' New students were connected to the tradition and community life of the college through participating in ancient rituals and customs.

On the other hand, Cambridge was also the crucible for great scientific developments. A few yards away was the Cavendish Laboratory where Rutherford had split the atom. When I was a student in the 1950s, though we didn't know it at the time, in the same laboratory, Crick and his colleagues were discovering the structure of DNA.

Cambridge had therefore two faces: 'Remembering' and 'Venturing Out'. The lesson from Isaiah 51 this morning, and indeed the whole of the last section of Isaiah, is also about 'Remembering' and 'Venturing Out'. Isaiah was preparing the people for the return home from exile after fifty years in Babylon. Some of the people scoffed and didn't want to move; some were afraid; others said God had abandoned them. Isaiah had a two-pronged message. His first theme was 'Remember the tradition': 'Look to the rock from which you were hewn and to the quarry from which you were dug. Look to Abraham your father and to Sarah who bore you.' Remember, hang onto all that God has done for you in the past, through which he has revealed his character. However, Isaiah didn't only try to galvanise the people by reminding them of the past; he spoke of God's actions *now*. Earlier, God had said to him: 'I am about to do a new thing . . . I will make a way in the wilderness and rivers in the desert' (43:19). 'Remembering' and 'Venturing Out'.

Today some people resolve the tension between tradition and modernity using one of two simple solutions. Some say nothing must change. Others say everything must change – the past is dead and has nothing to teach us. Was Jesus a traditionalist or an innovator? Well, he was both. He was a traditionalist in the sense that he was steeped in the Hebrew Scriptures and tradition; he was at the synagogue every Sabbath and in the Temple for all the important festivals. When he challenged people about their views about marriage or sacrifice, he appealed to an older tradition which had been forgotten. Again and again what was new and innovative about Jesus was not what he said but that he actually lived out elements in the tradition that had previously been mere words on the page. There is much about justice for the poor and outcast in the Old Testament. Jesus outraged people by putting it into practice.

The actress Joanna Lumley would perhaps be surprised to be mentioned in a sermon. I was intrigued to discover in her autobiography (*No Room for Secrets*, 2004) how she had reacted to her education in an Anglican convent school near Hastings. She had thoroughly enjoyed it, was moved by the worship, and admired the nuns. But she said that she didn't go to church now because the services had all changed. Religion was timeless. In 2012 she publicly joined others to celebrate the 350th anniversary of the 1662 Prayer Book. She felt that religion was 'mysterious' and the 'strange beauty of the old language' better expressed 'the inexplicable splendours and hopes that we address in church services'. What she overlooked was that the Prayer Book in its time was also shockingly new. Many of the changes in both Anglican and Roman Catholic worship during the last few years have actually been attempts to recover earlier traditions which had been lost. People say, 'I don't like this newfangled giving of the Peace.' Yet the Peace is a return to what early Christians did. The Reformation threw out many popular forms of devotion like statues, candles, ashes on Ash Wednesday, palms on Palm Sunday, feet washing on Maundy Thursday. Over the last century we have brought them back. Often what seems new is a recovery of tradition.

L.P. Hartley's novel *The Go-Between* famously begins 'The past is a foreign country. They do things differently there.' Precisely. Learning another language or visiting another culture challenges our self-centredness and our insularity. G.K. Chesterton wrote: 'tradition is only democracy extended through time. . . . Tradition may be defined as an extension of the franchise. Tradition means giving votes to the most obscure of all classes, our ancestors. It is the democracy of the dead' (*Orthodoxy*, 37). Taking seriously what believers in earlier centuries have thought and believed is to regard them as having the same value before

God as ourselves. When you go to buy a washing machine you want the latest model, but it's not like that with religion. Rather, religion is like wine, better for maturing. We need rootedness and solidarity. Knowing and valuing the history of the church is a bit like valuing and knowing the family photograph albums. Hence the great value of the creeds – they are wonderful hymns of praise for God who is revealed in what he has done and is doing.

The Holy Spirit has a great capacity to draw out new things from tradition. We saw on television recently how young sceptics who stayed for some weeks at the very traditional monastery at Worth had their lives changed. Brian Sewell, the sharp-tongued art critic, has been describing on television how he joined the deeply traditional pilgrimage to Santiago. At the end of his fifteen hundred mile journey he said he had discovered that 'centuries old teachings remained etched into my tortured and sceptical soul and I am glad for it'.

When a scientist makes a new discovery, in a sense it is not new at all. What the scientist sees at that moment of discovery has been there all the time – but either the scientific community has never noticed it, has excluded it due to previous theories or has lacked the apparatus to investigate it. For centuries Christians took slavery for granted; then two hundred years ago we looked at it with new eyes and declared it un-Christian. A century or more ago, Christians, trying to apply their faith to politics, for the first time began to see the Eucharist, the heart of the church's tradition, as a new vision of what society should be. Seventy-five years ago, the bishops of the Anglican Communion changed their minds about contraception. This change gave a new significance to one of the ancient purposes of marriage, as expressed in the 1662 Prayer Book Marriage Service: 'It was ordained for the mutual society, help, and comfort, that the one ought to have of the other, both in prosperity and adversity.'

Today we are wrestling with questions of gender: the role of women in the life and ministry of the church, and the nature of sexuality. So, like Isaiah, we look to the rock from which we were hewn.

# 47.
# Believing in God

You come into church one Sunday. You suddenly think as the Creed begins, 'Do I really believe in God? Perhaps it's all nonsense, a huge charade.' Or you watch the news and see hundreds of people dead after an earthquake, a war, a famine. Or you saw the programmes about the dinosaurs and asked 'Where was God when they were tearing each other apart?' A hundred years ago, Charles Gore was a canon at Westminster Abbey. He was also a well-known theologian. He used to say that there is only one very difficult Christian doctrine – that God is love. But for many of us, sometimes the problem is not simply whether God is love, but whether the world is so mad and so bad that it seems ludicrous to say 'I believe in God' at all.

My own belief is sometimes weaker and sometimes stronger. I guess that your belief ebbs and flows, too. The fact is that the world is ambiguous. We can collect one lot of evidence that points to the existence and the love of God, but a whole lot of other evidence points to agnosticism or atheism. Neither faith nor atheism fit all the evidence. If all the evidence pointed one way there would be no room for faith, for faith is not proof but an interpretation of the evidence, a way of seeing the world. It is not a way of answering all the questions. Nevertheless, faith seems to me to fit with more of the evidence than atheism. We should remember that a struggle to believe is quite normal; indeed, healthy. The Spanish philosopher Miguel de Unamuno wrote, 'Those who believe that they believe in God, but without passion in the heart, without anguish of mind, without uncertainty, without doubt, and even, at times, without despair, believe only in the idea of God, not in God himself.' What do you do, when your doubts overwhelm you? When doubts overwhelm me, I look in three directions: to God, to Jesus, to religious experience.

*1.*

I think that in some sense I have always believed in God, because I have always been conscious of the mystery surrounding us.

When I was six, we moved from Liverpool to a remote Welsh border village. I remember one winter evening waiting with my mother in a lane, deep in the country in total darkness. I had never experienced such total darkness before, not a light anywhere from a street lamp or a house. I clutched my mother's hand. I was not frightened; rather, I was awed by the vastness and mystery. Then the headlights of my father's car began to pierce the darkness of the road in the valley. He drew up, we got in, and all was normal again.

The mystery of life: it is extraordinary that we are here at all; that we are conscious of being here. It is amazing that when we investigate the world around us it is intelligible, as though it is the product of another mind. We are often anguished by the problems created by evil, suffering, and disasters. From time to time, people ask newscasters: 'For once, give us some good news.' But the evil of much news is a curious witness to the fact that much of the news is actually good. We never hear, 'The NatWest bank in Westminster has not been robbed today.' No one thinks of announcing, 'Today, 13 February, water is still $H_2O$.' Despite all the illnesses we suffer, we continue to speak of them as departures from the norm – we call them diseases or illnesses. It forces me to ponder not only the evil done by human beings but also their courage and resilience in the most appalling circumstances.

I am struck particularly by the way that humour always keeps breaking through. A couple of years ago I spoke at a conference about death. Lionel Blue was one of the speakers. He told the story of a group of old Jewish men discussing whom they would like to lie next to when they died. One said Sigmund Freud; another, David Ben-Gurion. Then a little man broke in, 'I'd like to lie next to Betty Cohen.' The rest protested: 'Betty Cohen is still alive!' 'That's the whole point,' said the little man.

What kind of people are we, what kind of a world is it, that we joke even about our own deaths? Then I read that there are half a trillion stars in our galaxy alone, and over half a trillion galaxies in the observable universe, and awe takes over. Thus we experience the universe as both meaning and mystery. Both meaning and mystery renew my faith. The universe is mysterious, yet our minds can comprehend something of it. I find that belief in God, however difficult, fits more of the facts of experience than atheism.

## 2.

When my faith is challenged and tested, I turn to look at Jesus. I have
taught other faiths for the Open University, and grown to admire many
aspects of them. Yet I believe that Jesus is the word of God made flesh
– and made fresh. He did not find faith easy in the wilderness or in the
garden of Gethsemane. On the cross he cried, 'My God, my God, why
have you forsaken me?'

It is as though just when we have got everything sized up and organised
and explained, in comes Jesus doing cartwheels, a clown-like figure –
remember how Charlie Chaplin looked so unimportant, so powerless?
Yet Jesus put down the mighty from their seat and exalted the humble
and meek as we heard sung a few minutes ago in the Magnificat. Jesus
says, 'Just when you think you've arrived, I'll blow up the station, just
when you think you've got onto high table, I'll show you that those who
think they are in, are out, and those who think they are out, are really in.'
Then there is his extraordinary love – we look at him staggering along
the road to Calvary and we dare to say, 'He did that for us, he did that for
me.' We hear his words at the Eucharist: 'This is my body, given for you.'
When my faith is ebbing and flickering, I begin to believe again through
that strange young man on his cross, as George Tyrrell called him. When
my faith is threatened, I recall the mystery of life which points to God; I
refresh my faith with the liveliness of Jesus.

## 3.

I also reflect upon my own religious experience. I know that saying the
daily offices of Morning and Evening Prayer, and finding time to be
silent before God makes a huge difference to me. If I get slack about
praying, I feel hungry, as though I have missed a meal. Sometimes I feel
that God is absent when I pray, but as R.S. Thomas, the priest and poet,
says in 'The Absence', the pain of his absence is a kind of presence. I have
discovered that after a long time of this apparent absence, God suddenly
makes himself known in a vivid way and then vanishes again. Again,
as I have ministered the sacraments as a priest, I have seen them work.
I have seen so many people go away free from their burdens, having
made their confessions and having heard me say, 'And by his authority
committed unto me I absolve you from all your sins.' I reflect that as I
live the drama of the Christian year, each season proves to be true in
experience – people and situations are redeemed through suffering, I
and other people do experience resurrection.

'At present we see only puzzling reflections in a mirror, but one day we shall see face to face,' says St Paul (I Corinthians 13:12). In the meantime, we have glimpses of glory. Alan Ecclestone, a remarkable priest in Sheffield, once described his visit to a steelworker who got up every morning at four o'clock to bird watch on the outskirts, before he went to his six a.m. shift. Once he saw a hawk. That was a glimpse of glory. In between these rare sightings he searched the woods and fields for birds' feathers. He collected them into a tin box and when Alan Ecclestone called, he got out his tin box and showed them to him and turned them over as though they were pure gold.

In this life we only have rare sightings of God himself, but we can treasure those traces, those signs, those glimpses which he gives us day by day. 'At present we see only puzzling reflections in a mirror, but one day we shall see face to face.' May it be so. Amen.

# 48.
# Anglican-Roman Catholic Relations

If you break a plate in two, it is not too difficult to stick it back together again. It's much more difficult to repair it if there are several breaks. Mending plates is easier than mending relationships, especially between whole communities, as we know from Northern Ireland. When relationships break down between individuals or communities, there are often bitterness, anger, and recriminations; there is a tendency to think of the other party as the enemy and the one to blame for the breakdown. Yet people sometimes escape from the caricatures that bedevil the breakdowns of relationships. A divorced wife remarked with amazement: 'When Bill was married to me he never lifted a finger around the house. Since he married Mary I hear he hoovers the house from top to bottom without being asked.'

The Week of Prayer for Christian Unity began yesterday. It is based on the text from John 17:21, where Jesus prayed 'that they may all be one. As you, Father, are in me and I am in you, may they also be in us, so that the world may believe that you have sent me.' This morning I want to concentrate upon Anglican-Roman Catholic relations: partly because I haven't the time to cover the whole ecumenical scene; partly because our two cathedrals in Portsmouth are so close physically; partly because the Roman Catholic and Anglican churches are more like one another than any other two churches: both are episcopal, both liturgical; both value the Eucharist as the main act of worship; both exercise the same seven sacramental ministries.

During and after the quarrels of the Reformation period, we both grew apart and developed separately – sometimes in reaction against one another. Because Anglicans now had their services in English, English Roman Catholics vowed that they would always stick to Latin. Because some in the Middle Ages had treated statues superstitiously, for some considerable time, Anglicans wouldn't have any statues at all. It reminds me of the story of the Anglican priest who put a statue of Mary in the parish church. An angry parishioner protested: 'We don't want any dead Roman Catholics in our church.'

Before about 1960, English Roman Catholics kept themselves apart. They were told not even to step inside the church of another allegiance. When I became a Cambridge college chaplain in 1961, the Roman Catholic chaplain at the university refused to have any contact with any Anglican chaplains. Up to 1949, Roman Catholics were not allowed even to say the Lord's Prayer with other Christians.

When a new Roman Catholic chaplain arrived, he reflected the new spirit generated by the Second Vatican Council, then meeting in Rome. He at once joined the weekly meetings of college chaplains. From time to time I was now able to ask Roman Catholic priests to preach after Sunday Evensong. Roman Catholic students joined the college ecumenical study groups. The most obvious changes happened when Roman Catholics and Anglicans began to revise their liturgies in consultation with each other. The new Roman Catholic and Anglican Eucharists were so similar that many laypeople could not distinguish between them. In the old days one was in Latin, the other in Tudor English, and each had a rather different shape. Both Anglican and Roman Catholic laypeople in the past had tended to treat Eucharistic worship as a background to their private devotions; now both churches stressed the communal and participative nature of the new liturgies. Indeed, Roman Catholic worship could now be sometimes more simple than Anglican worship. One Easter, a friend of mine, a leading evangelical Anglican liturgist, went to both of his local cathedrals, Roman Catholic and Anglican. He found Roman Catholic worship more evangelical.

There has been a convergence in worship. Much good has happened since that first visit of an Archbishop of Canterbury to Rome in 1960. But something went wrong. There were those Anglicans and Roman Catholics who blamed it all on Anglicans for ordaining women priests. This ignores the considerable support for the ordination of women among Roman Catholics. The slackening of progress began as the Vatican seized back power from the bishops. Two conservative popes hardly thought Anglican-Roman Catholic unity a priority. The Anglican-Roman Catholic International Commission was created by Pope Paul and Archbishop Ramsey in 1966 to work at old problems with fresh language. Using this approach, the Commission reported in 1981 a remarkable convergence in doctrine. However, the Vatican took ten years to come up with an authoritative response. Some Roman Catholics insisted that this doctrinal harmony in new language was not enough, and that Anglicans must agree to the traditional formulations. A conservative spirit was spreading across all churches as they were faced with declining attendances and the growth of independent charismatic congregations. Some church leaders were so intent on keeping the individual ships afloat that they considered ecumenism a distraction. Why not settle down and accept divisions? There are two main reasons.

1. The church is intended to be a model community showing the world how peoples of different outlooks, races, temperaments and nationalities can live together creatively, enriching one another. There is one baptism, one Eucharist. There should not be two bishops in Portsmouth.
2. We also need one another's insights and perspectives. A divided church cannot serve the whole nation out of its own resources of wisdom and tradition when these are limited by division. Unity and mission belong together.

What should we do? I suggest that there should be two types of activity, possible even though we are divided, not least about the papacy. We should be face to face and shoulder to shoulder.

To begin with, a few members of our two cathedral congregations in Portsmouth know one another. From time to time, we worship in each other's churches. We could draw upon the wisdom and knowledge of the association of inter-church families to help those in mixed marriages. Certainly Anglicans regard Roman Catholicism as too authoritarian. To take an example: an Asian theologian was excommunicated for questioning papal infallibility and for supporting the ordination of women. Anglicans often go to the other extreme by being individualistic, with little sense of the church beyond the local parish and little interest in the worldwide Anglican Communion. Yet both our churches are coalitions. Recently, a well-known Roman Catholic nun preached at the ordination of women priests at St Asaph Cathedral in Wales.

Secondly, it is when Christians face outwards that they find themselves side by side and united. Some areas of Portsmouth are said to be amongst the poorest in the south of England. What could the churches do together to help the poor, the unemployed, drug addicts, alienated young people, racial minorities who feel marginalised, and refugees awaiting decisions about their future?

I will leave you with a final picture, created by Cardinal Hume when he was enthroned at Westminster Cathedral in 1976. He walked from Westminster Cathedral to Westminster Abbey, where Anglican and Roman Catholic monks sang Vespers together. In his sermon he said: 'We have been, I think, like two sisters – estranged, not on speaking terms, quarrelsome, misunderstanding each other.' He reminded the congregation that one tomb in the Abbey contained the remains of two sisters, Elizabeth and Mary. He said: 'Read there the inscription: "Consorts both in throne and grave, here we rest, two sisters, Elizabeth and Mary in the hope of resurrection."'

# 49.
# Interpreting the Bible

When I was thirteen, I was told at school that we were going to study Macbeth. That year I was given a complete Shakespeare for Christmas. I looked through the text of Macbeth we were studying at school. I discovered that our school text had been censored – anything to do with sex was omitted and some of the most vivid curses by the witches had been toned down. The witches had been turned into polite old ladies at a tea party. This all took place in the mid-1940s, when society was more decorous. Today, we cannot imagine any third former being shocked by Shakespeare. In the Lent Term, pupils at a leading public school staged the notorious Jacobean play '*Tis Pity She's a Whore*.

The Church of England claims that it daily reads more of the Bible publicly day by day than any other church. Yet the Church of England censors Scripture. Stories of incest, rape and those long genealogical lists are omitted. Sometimes brutal incidents are regarded as too awful to be read. We read in 1 Samuel 15 the story of the capture of Agag, king of the Amalekites. The lesson ends with Samuel denouncing Agag. Our lectionary omits the following verse, verse 33: 'And Samuel hewed Agag in pieces before the Lord in Gilgal.' Was that deemed too nasty for Anglican ears at Evensong?

Anaesthetics began to be used in childbirth in the nineteenth century. Conservative Christians quoted Genesis 3:16 against it: 'I will greatly increase your pangs in childbearing: in pain you shall bring forth children.' The supporters of chloroform also quoted the Genesis story of how God put Adam into a deep sleep when he operated on Adam to bring forth Eve. (Genesis 2:31) What eventually decided the issue? It became known that Queen Victoria had been given chloroform during the birth of Prince Leopold in 1853, so, ironically, it was Queen Victoria, not the church, who settled the dispute.

Tonight we had a fascinating act of censorship by those who compile the lectionary. The second lesson was taken from the letter to Titus 2:1-8, 11-14. Titus probably became the first bishop of Crete. This passage gives standard moral advice to each section of a first century Christian household. It begins with how older men and older women should behave, and prescribes the behaviour of husbands, wives and children, as well as younger men and slaves. The two verses about slaves, 9-10, were omitted from the lectionary. What do the omitted verses say? 'Tell slaves to be submissive to their masters and to give satisfaction in every respect; they are not to answer back, not to pilfer, but to show complete and perfect fidelity, so that in everything they may be an ornament to the doctrine of God our Saviour.'

Now, why did the compilers of the lectionary omit those two verses? Because modern households don't include slaves? On that basis you'd omit any mention of kings in a republic like Ireland. Was it omitted out of embarrassment? Is the church embarrassed to admit that the Bible simply takes the institution of slavery for granted? For seventeen hundred years Christians were quite happy to go on reading biblical passages which accepted slavery. Those who regarded the bible as infallible took it literally as the Word of God. What changed and why? Why, after seventeen hundred years during which Christians believed that they should support slavery, did they change their minds? Why did they see Scripture as bearing witness against slavery? In the eighteenth century Christians began to think that God could lead us into new directions; that God could speak a new Word to us. Those Christians who argued for the abolition of slavery searched the Scriptures for texts against slavery but found none. Everywhere in the Old and New Testaments slavery was assumed to be part of the divine order. In the passage from Titus which was excluded from our second lesson, therefore, it was quite natural to include a passage about how slaves should behave in a Christian household. The abolitionists could not quote texts against slavery, so they appealed to the broader principle of love. They also appealed to experience. Granville Sharp became a keen Christian abolitionist because he saw a slave awaiting medical treatment for savage wounds inflicted by his owner.

What do we learn from the story of how slavery was abolished? That evidence from Scripture can be ambiguous. We learn that complex issues cannot be resolved by appealing to individual texts. We learn that conscience isn't a monopoly of Christians. Those Christians who were abolitionists often had their consciences sharpened by exchanges with agnostics and humanists.

The story of how Christians changed their minds about slavery could help us to tackle more fairly relationships between people of the same sex. Those Christians who today advocate a change of mind about same-sex relationships are accused of being dominated by secular values. Similar accusations were thrown at the abolitionists. It was the spreading of liberal values that paved the way for the abolition of slavery. The abolitionists were a coalition between liberal and conservative Christians that included humanists and agnostics.

Today, a coalition that includes a considerable number of Christians believes that it would be right for the church as well as the state to recognise publicly bonds between people of the same sex. Faithful commitment of every kind is vital to the stability of any society. Opponents of such a change point to certain texts in the Bible, just as those opposed to the abolition of slavery pointed to many biblical texts which supported slavery. When we look at the Bible as a whole, however, it is about the faithful commitment of God through thick and thin to the human race. Some who experienced the brutality of slavery changed their minds and supported its abolition. Similarly, today an increasing number of Christians change their minds as they experience the fidelity and love of committed same-sex relationships. Such relationships would be strengthened by the blessing and prayers of the church.

We began by wondering why the church tonight omitted those verses about slavery from tonight's lesson. It has given us an opportunity to remember that Christians after seventeen centuries were prepared to change their minds about slavery. As we recall that, we can understand why significant numbers of Christians today believe that we should change our attitude to same-sex relationships. This would be a new departure. It was a new departure when Christians campaigned against slavery, even though slavery was unanimously supported by Scripture and church tradition. From this story, we should learn that we should always test every text from Scripture against the character of Jesus, the Word of God.

# 50.
# Jericho and Tribal Religion

Now the gates of Jericho were securely barred because of the Israelites. No one went out and no one came in. Then the Lord said to Joshua, 'See, I have delivered Jericho into your hands, along with its king and its fighting men. March around the city once with all the armed men. Do this for six days. Have seven priests carry trumpets of rams' horns in front of the ark. On the seventh day, march around the city seven times, with the priests blowing the trumpets. When you hear them sound a long blast on the trumpets, have the whole army give a loud shout; then the wall of the city will collapse and the army will go up, everyone straight in.'

*Joshua 6:1-5*

What did you make of the first lesson about Joshua and Jericho? (Joshua 5:13-6:20.) Did you really hear God speaking through it? Or did you just treat it as a vividly told adventure story? Or perhaps you switched off? In that case, I will summarise.

First, let us set it in its context. Every nation has its national sagas, stories by which it defines itself. England tells the stories of King Alfred, Queen Elizabeth and the Armada, Queen Victoria and the Empire, Churchill and the Second World War. Very often such events have been regarded as God's blessing on our nation. We were sometimes asked to believe in a tribal, national God who specially favoured us. So, too, with Israel. They believed themselves specially called by God. God had shown his favour by rescuing them from slavery in Egypt, by preserving them in their pilgrimage through the desert, by keeping them safe when carried off into captivity in Babylon, by enabling them to rebuild Jerusalem and re-establish the nation when they returned. Again and again, the Old Testament writers and psalmists return to celebrate these sagas.

This is where tonight's lesson from Joshua fits in. Having escaped from slavery in Egypt, the people are marching on, led by Joshua to the Promised Land, capturing city after city. They come to Jericho. Joshua has a vision of the angel commander of the Lord's army to assure him of God's support. God tells Joshua to march round the city for six days with seven priests bearing seven trumpets (seven was a sacred number). On the seventh day, the trumpets were to sound and the people were to give a great shout and the walls would tumble down. They obeyed and the walls fell down.

But our lesson omitted the verse at the end which describes what happened next: 'Then they devoted to destruction by the end of the sword all in the city, both men and women, young and old, oxen, sheep and donkeys.' (Joshua 6:21.) Those who select the lessons for the Church of England obviously thought it would be unedifying for us to hear about this indiscriminate slaughter by God's chosen people, especially as it was regarded as an offering to God, which he wanted to receive. Those who during the Second World War defended the indiscriminate bombing of Germany at least did not regard it as an offering to God which he required. This story raises lots of problems. Did the collapse of the walls have a natural explanation? Was it the result of an earth tremor? Modern excavation suggests that Jericho was little more than a fort.

All this is to miss the point of the story, the telling of which was motivated by a desire to prove that God was on their side, as he was during the Exodus. Even so, there are bigger problems raised by this story. How can the picture of God in this story be reconciled with what we know of God in Jesus, the Jesus who in tonight's lesson (Matthew 11:20-end) tells us, 'Come to me, all you that are weary and carrying heavy burdens, and I will give you rest. Take my yoke upon you, and learn from me, for I am gentle and humble in heart, and you will find rest for your souls.' (11:28-9.) By contrast, the God of Joshua was a tribal God – and a God of war.

As we move on in the Old Testament, however, we see how God educated his people to shed such primitive ideas about himself. When Jerusalem is besieged, the prophet Jeremiah actually sees the foreign besiegers as the instruments of God's judgement on a faithless city. In Isaiah, King Cyrus of Persia is described as God's anointed. The prophet Malachi pictures true worship arising from every nation: 'From the rising of the sun to its setting my name is great among the nations, and in every place incense is offered to my name.' (1:11.) Two of the most arresting figures in the Old Testament, Job and Ruth, were not Jews at all. Gradually, God brought the Jews to realise that, though they had a special calling, God is the creator of the world and all peoples; he is not a tribal God. He is not a God who delights in destruction but one who loves and values all peoples.

What does it all matter? Isn't it old, dead history? No. We have seen in the last few years the terrible results of bad religion – whether in Northern Ireland between Christian tribes or in religiously-inspired terrorism. Passages like the one we heard about Jericho have surely influenced the policy of Israel since 1948. Israel's army has destroyed hundreds of Arab villages and expelled their inhabitants to make room for Israelis. Or again: I was having my hair cut when the news came through over the radio in the shop that the bombing of the Twin Towers had been done by deeply religious people. The hairdresser was so furious that I thought he was going to cut all my hair off. He said: 'All religion is evil – it only produces conflict and violence.'

In our own country, there was a big change in attitude for the Church of England between the two world wars. In the First World War, there were quite a lot of Joshuas about, Christians who regarded God as our own tribal English god. By the Second World War, Anglicans were a lot less tribal. They realised that in the creeds we do not affirm our belief in the Church of England but in the Holy Catholic Church, which includes people of all nations and races. When war was declared at 11 a.m. on 3 September 1939, the news was brought into Chichester Cathedral. George Bell, the bishop there, had been working tirelessly to house German refugees who had fled because they were Jews. He knew how evil Nazism was, but he had also built up many deep relationships with Christians in Germany. As the news was announced, Bishop Bell left his stall in the cathedral and walked quietly to the altar and reminded the congregation that they were to be Christians, to have pity on their enemies and throughout the war to have forgiveness in their hearts.

In November 1940, Vera Brittain, the pacifist writer (and mother of Shirley Williams) visited St Paul's Cathedral, with its altar area shattered by a bomb. She was given a booklet of prayers and was relieved to discover that it expressed penitence for Britain's sins and included this prayer: 'From bitterness and vindictiveness against our enemies, from persecution and suspicion of refugees and aliens: Good Lord deliver us.'

When Coventry was heavily bombed, hundreds were killed one night in November 1940 and many churches, including the cathedral, were destroyed. On the morning after the raid, charred beams from the roof were tied in the form of a cross and planted in a mound of rubble. The Cathedral Provost in a Christmas broadcast said in a service from the ruins: 'We are trying, hard as it may be, to banish all thoughts of revenge.'

An altar was built and the Provost caused an inscription to be carved: 'Father Forgive'. He explained that it did not mean 'forgive them' (for no one is innocent) but 'forgive us all'. This began the Coventry Cathedral ministry of reconciliation, which is directed especially towards Germany. It still continues seventy years later.

Through these stories, we realise that we've come a long way from the tribal god of war in whom Joshua believed. However, there are still those who still believe in a tribal god and a tribal church. It is salutary to remember that most Anglicans are not white and don't live in England but in Africa. Anglicans are also to be found in unexpected places like Korea, Japan and South America – none of which has received much English influence. Jesus is the Greek version of the name Joshua. Tonight's first lesson prompts us to ask: who we are to follow, Joshua or Jesus? Which one reveals the true nature of God?

# If you enjoyed this book, why not try...

## The Church of England and the First World War

### Alan Wilkinson

ISBN: 9780718893217
PDF ISBN: 9780718841645
ePub ISBN: 9780718841652
Kindle ISBN: 9780718841669

*The Church of England and the First World War* (first published in 1978) explores in depth the role of the Church during the tragic circumstances of the First World War using biographies, newspapers, magazines, letters, poetry and other sources in a balanced evaluation.

The myth that the war was fought by 'lions led by donkeys' powerfully endures – it turns heroes into victims. Alan Wilkinson demonstrates the sheer horror, moral ambiguity, and the interaction between religion, the Church and war with a scholarly, and yet poetic, hand. The author creates a vivid image of the Church and society, the views of the Free Church and Roman Catholics, the pastoral problems presented by war, the traditions born of imperialistic British history, and the urges for reform.

*The Church of England and the First World War* is written with compassion and great historical understanding, making the book hard to put down. This expert and classic study will grip the religious and secular alike, the general reader or the student.

# Dissent or Conform?

*War, Peace and the English Churches 1900-1945*

## Alan Wilkinson

ISBN: 9780718892074

*Dissent or Conform?* examines how churches reacted to, and were affected by, the two world wars. Its underlying theme, however, is how the Church can be a creatively dissenting community, focusing on how easily the church can turn into a conforming community that only encourages the occurrence of uncreative dissenters, the ones who criticise the power without offering solutions which lead to a real change.

Wilkinson opposes this trait of the church, especially given the impact that it has on society as a messenger of the Gospel. To this end, the author depicts religious groups during three periods of time: English Nonconformity among the free churches before WWI, pacifists and pacifiers between the two wars and Christianity during WWII, focussing on how church history interacts with the developments in history and society.

This book is of particular interest to social and church historians of the twentieth century, and to all interested in the history and ethics of war and pacifism. It will also appeal to those interested in the interaction between church and society.

*Available now with more excellent titles in Paperback, Hardback, PDF and Epub formats from The Lutterworth Press.*

#0006 - 121217 - C0 - 234/156/10 - PB - 9780718894986